LIFERIDER

LIFER

HEART, BODY, SOUL, **AND** LIFE BEYOND THE OCEAN

LAIRD
HAMILTON

with Julian Borra

RODALE.
New York

Copyright © 2019 by Laird Hamilton

All rights reserved.
Published in the United States by Rodale Books,
an imprint of the Crown Publishing Group,
a division of Penguin Random House LLC, New York.
crownpublishing.com
rodalebooks.com

RODALE and the Plant colophon are
registered trademarks of Penguin Random House LLC.

Library of Congress Cataloging-in-Publication Data
is available upon request.

ISBN 978-1-63565-290-1
eISBN 978-1-63565-291-8

PRINTED IN THE UNITED STATES OF AMERICA

Book design by Andrea Lau
Photographs by Jennifer Cawley
Jacket design by Cardon Webb
Jacket photograph by Jennifer Cawley

10 9 8 7 6 5 4 3 2 1

First Edition

I have no belief
But I believe
I'm a walking contradiction
And I ain't got no right

—GREEN DAY, "WALKING CONTRADICTION"

I sent my Soul through the Invisible,
Some letter of that After-life to spell:
And by and by my Soul return'd to me,
And answer'd "I Myself am Heav'n and Hell"

—*THE RUBAIYAT OF OMAR KHAYYAM,*
TRANSLATED BY EDWARD FITZGERALD

We're all so busy looking for something
Looking for some Aha moment
But you know,
We were in the Aha moment
We *were* the Aha moment
And then we got knowledge;
And we slowly moved further and further
away from things.

—LAIRD HAMILTON

CONTENTS

LIFERIDER

INTRODUCTION

IT would be very easy to dismiss Laird Hamilton.

Many have. And still do.

Controversial. Incorrigible. Radical. Visionary. Revolutionary. Disrespectful. Disobedient. Unpredictable. A dick.

Laird's emphatic statement that he would "take every wave, and don't get in my way. Big dogs eat first" set him up as a potentially extraordinary yet fairly unpleasant growing master of his art.

Playing Lance Burkhart in the seminal '80s surf movie *North Shore* didn't exactly help his burgeoning reputation as a bad boy.

Even positive comments, as celebratory as they are, seem to be in some ways still intent on putting him back in a box.

There are many people who view Laird Hamilton as a force

of nature. His last book was titled exactly that. Whether Laird's tongue was at this point firmly in his own or someone else's cheek is not clear. (Laird is surprisingly humble about himself.)

But for many people, when they watch a YouTube clip, or look at a magazine spread, or hear a podcast, they simply see and hear a slightly folksy, big wave culture; a lifestyle of fitness routines and superfoods; and a surfer narcissism of "wave first" always.

This is to some extent understandable. The internet is teeming with Lairdness and Lairdisms. Laird's aphorisms are everywhere.

But there's a lot more to Laird than meets the eye. And to dismiss him as mostly irrelevant to us "land-based" folk, or to park him as some type of Peter Pan figure, is to miss something.

In some ways Laird is like the waves he rides. Seemingly simple. Yet intriguingly complex.

Liferider is a small journey into that.

Liferider is Laird's view from the lip of life; observations from where he is right now on how we might better manage the turbulence of life—the biggest wave we'll ever ride—by reaching back into the brilliant creature we are, instead of always reaching up to the being we aspire to be.

If *Force of Nature* captured Laird, the *he'e nalu*—the Wave Slider—by skimming *across* the surface and sheen of the lifestyle of one of the world's greatest big wave surfers, *Liferider* is the foil that taps into the energy *inside* his wave. To reach a little deeper, and range a little wider, through the brilliant creature that is Laird Hamilton.

"Brilliant creature" is not a grand title only to be applied to a celebrity surfer, it is the *Liferider* term for who and what we are at our best.

Laird believes we're all brilliant creatures, and that we have only just started to tap into the amazing human organism that we are.

When you strip everything back, down to the most basic elements of our species, we as humans can draw on an extraordinarily sophisticated and delicately calibrated combination of physicality, intelligence, emotion, and intuition, at both the conscious and the unconscious level. Our human consciousness lights us up in a way no other species comes close to matching.

In talks with school children, Laird inspires them to take a closer, harder look at the Brilliant Creatures that they are.

"You can run, swim, dive, fly. You are amazing. You have untapped potential in you that would blow your mind."

—LAIRD HAMILTON

In this also lies one of the truths of *Liferider.*

While the world increasingly seeks happiness in memes and self-help books—millions of us reaching upward every day toward some enlightened being that we wish to be—Laird is more intent on inspiring us to reach back into the primal organism, the brilliant creature we are: to unlock those doors, throw some of those genetic switches, and mine more of ourselves *for* ourselves.

Liferider is not against enlightenment. It simply seeks to inspire us to be the best and most brilliant creature that we can be, seen through the lens of Laird. Starting with the physical organism.

The simple premise of *Liferider* is this: start with the groundwork.

Be the best or fittest organism you can be. Build the best

foundation you can from which to then pursue whatever enlightenment or elevation you might desire.

And *movement* is a keystone of that foundation. Call it exercise. Call it keeping fit. Call it evolution. Call it getting off your ass and doing something. Call it whatever you like. But movement is a crucial part of that groundwork. In order to think, we need to move.

We are built for movement. Movement defines us as creatures.

When we forget to move, we lose momentum. We forget our most basic selves. When our thinking starts to overwhelm our doing, that is not always a good thing.

Less thinking; more doing.

That is how we evolve and continue to grow.

This means movement of every kind—physical, intellectual, emotional, and spiritual.

In the words of the galactic funkster George Clinton and his seminal funk rock troupe, Parliament-Funkadelic, "free your mind and your ass will follow."

Our minds are so consumed these days. We're busy. Busy, busy, busy. And we're feeding our brains a tsunami of stimulus every day. We're screenagers, hopping from device to device, consuming the all-you-can-eat, byte-sized buffet of social networks and the connected self.

Technology has created in us a new layer of digital consciousness that enhances and amplifies almost every aspect of our lives; but to a certain degree we are becoming trapped by it. It has become another barrier between ourselves and the brilliant creatures we are.

As we have developed as a species, we have always put up barriers between ourselves and the natural world in which we have evolved. Shelters, walls, windows, roofs, heat. Each layer a new man-made skin.

Staggering invention and innovation have made us the pre-eminent creature on the planet.

And over the most recent millennia, our minds have gone into overdrive, using the technologies of language, mechanics, engineering, printing; still and moving pictures; telecommunication; and now, digital platforms, networks, and artificial intelligence to propagate the memes of human evolution, and in the process sharing and spreading the word on how to be better and more civilized.

What About Mindfulness?

Technological progress has allowed us to surge forward as a species. But it also makes us lazy. We have used technology to move ourselves from a short life of incredible hardship to one that is far longer and now allows for increasing luxury. And with luxury comes pleasure and subsequently inertia.

We're using technology to find the path of least resistance, increasingly seeking a "frictionless world."

But friction and resistance are human needs. They are how we evolve. We thrive on them. And we need to keep them alive in us.

Laird is committed to creating friction. Putting the organism under duress.

Gabby Reece, his wife, goes further. She believes that Laird not only needs friction to exist. She would say he *is* friction. That is what he brings to the world around him.

Every aspect of their XPT (Extreme Performance Training) course focuses on stressing the physical, the mental, and the spiritual in every participant—taking them *beyond*.

That's what Laird does.

He has spent a lifetime reaching beyond himself, beyond what is. Starting with his physicality.

Laird has a roadmap of injuries that plot his time on the planet doing what he does—stressing the organism. Pushing it beyond what it might seem capable of.

And one thing that he will share with anyone interested enough to ask is that at the heart of that is movement.

Movement—of our body, our mind, our emotions—shapes how we live.

Movement also shapes how we heal. We heal faster when we move. Even when every fiber in us is saying *please don't—it hurts*, healing through movement is engineered into us.

When risk and danger existed all around us, inertia was not an option. So we have evolved the ability to heal while we move. Because to *not* move once meant death.

And if we are engineered to do nothing else, we are engineered to survive—this is the gene pool imperative. Survive, stay alive, for as long as possible, to multiply the gene pool as often as possible. All of our nurture mechanisms—and so many of all our capabilities—initially stem from the organism's desire to stay alive.

Millennia before our enlightened age set in, millions of years were spent honing the organism in the natural world—to survive.

Liferider is an invitation to free your mind from itself, and from the all-consuming Information Age, even if just for a few hours a week, and move your proverbial ass. In any direction, in any way, to any degree, but move it nonetheless.

Natural Intelligence

Liferider has no interest in dismissing the advances of human existence.

Technology as we currently know it is an amazing thing. Social networks and hyper-connectivity are transforming human existence, creating paradigm shifts in social and cultural development.

Technology is raising whole societies out of poverty, liberating men and women across the world to achieve incredible things. It is reshaping democracy, enabling it to emerge in new forms that challenge and transform tyrannical regimes. It is accelerating understanding, innovation and implementation in health care and the study of diseases through the application of big data and AI in genomic and other sciences.

Technology is generating increasing yields, new sources, and startling innovations in food production and nutritional understanding.

Technology is simply amazing.

But AI and machine learning are turning the world we know upside down. They are substituting grinding tasks, once undertaken by millions of people, with intelligent, evolving algorithms that "think" for themselves.

To the programmers and coders and designers that create them, these technologies are awesome. To the ordinary person who quietly goes about their business in some back office, or on some production line, the same technologies are quietly terrifying.

The evolving nature and accelerating capability of AI are creating a crisis of identity in many of us.

We are losing our grip on what it is to be human. We are

becoming anxious and, to an increasing degree, scared of the capabilities of the machines we're creating.

As science fiction becomes science fact, and bots and artificial intelligence look to replace us, we find ourselves wondering about our role in the world.

We are struggling with our human identity, scared that our human self will fail us somehow—that we will be incapable of keeping up with our algorithmic machine replacements.

We're losing faith in ourselves as creatures.

In the midst of that doubt, that loss of faith, *Liferider* seeks to act as a counterpoint to the current culture, to remind us in some small way of what it is to be human. Really human. From the organism outward.

As we struggle to decipher our place between ancient and replicant, *Liferider* puts up a few signposts to help us along the way. As Laird explores his own feelings of what it is to be human—often at the most primitive level—he sheds light on what resides within us: a kaleidoscope of amazing competencies and capabilities from millennia of evolution, many of which have been left dormant: an internal intelligence that facilitates our ability to do extraordinary things.

Liferider intends to remind us that our intuitive "primal" selves are there, always, ticking along merrily.

Whether we realize it or not, in continuously switching between our conscious and unconscious selves—whether we're sitting in a traffic jam, in a boardroom, watching a movie, getting busy between the sheets, or raising hell at the theme park—we're switching between older and younger aspects of the evolving organism that we are.

And we are all the more brilliant for our ability to do that.

We do not necessarily need to do something extraordinary to trigger these deeper and sometimes dormant faculties. They don't require us to smash a wave, dive off a rock face, or fly through thin air to trigger them. There are many ways to provoke them into being.

In Laird's world, these capabilities and competencies are like seams of precious metal waiting to be mined and elevated into simple riches that can enhance our everyday life. And there are gifts and rewards for anyone who chooses to do so.

In reaching into the brilliant creature that we are, we become more resilient. We rebalance our conscious and unconscious minds in order to ride the turbulence of life better. And we remind ourselves that beyond the protein-based supercomputer that some trending scientists and academics would say we are—we are quite amazing.

While seeking a greater understanding of that brilliant creature, Laird believes, we might remind ourselves that we are profoundly connected to the natural world in which we have evolved—and to the creatures that we share this planet with—in ways far beyond the comprehension of science.

We might remember that mystery and wonder are two of the greatest evolutionary mechanisms in the human armory—the things that keep us reaching *beyond* ourselves.

We might remember what it is to be truly human.

The Human Hammock

You could be forgiven for thinking that the mysticism of the ancients is dead.

That the old modes of spirituality, focused on understanding the relationship between our physical and metaphysical selves, are increasingly being rendered redundant. Reason rules. The left brain shapes everything.

Dawkins, Hawking, Dennett, the masters of super-reasoning and left-brain dominance, rule the airwaves of human debate.

If appearances are to be believed, this left-brain ascendancy has left the right-brain crowd to twiddle their existential thumbs, sitting outside a café somewhere, leafing through texts rendered obsolete by the big bang of computing, the march of science, accelerating technology, and the tidal waves of big data that feed it.

Laird does not dismiss the unknown. Or assert the known.

Laird loves science. He's a nerd. He loves the engineering of life. Looking under the hood of himself and every other natural thing, to understand the mechanisms at work in the world.

But therein lies the contradiction of the man. Because although Laird doesn't do *fluffy* spiritualism, he believes in something bigger than himself. And comfortably so.

Laird happily exists between the known and the unknown.

In that way he is both the Christian and the Hawaiian islander of his upbringing; and the geek who designs aerodynamic foils.

There's a lot to read "between the lines" of Laird's physical and metaphysical selves.

You will find a simple Christianity at work in him. He references the Parables as texts by which to shape our actions, our morality, and our ethics.

He likes that the Parables are active, "doing" texts. Not dissimilar to the Hawaiian practice of "mindful action"—where you are taught through simple lessons to act in all things with consideration and consciousness.

But he doesn't do dogma. He wears his beliefs very lightly, and his Christianity seems to have been stitched almost seamlessly into and around other beliefs and understandings that hold equal merit and interest for him.

The one immutable given for Laird? *Connectedness to everything.* Far beyond that of smartphones, integrated platforms, APIs, and social networks, true connectedness defines his worldview.

Punk Contrarian

Laird's upbringing was neither smooth nor privileged.

He never knew his father. And his mother was actively part of the counterculture movement of the time, moving away from "society" as it was then, and placing herself and her son at the heart of the most countercultural movement there was: surfing.

> "The Hawaiians have a *hānai* system; *hānai* is another word for adopting; you take somebody in and you treat them as if they are your own.
>
> "My wife's family took him in, and taught him basic ways of life, how to survive, and Laird needed that—and they saw something special in him."
>
> —COPPIN COLBURN, HAMILTON FAMILY FRIEND

He arrived on the island at a raw age, a white, blond outsider in the midst of a culture reasserting itself in the world. Hawaiian culture was ascendant in the late 1960s and '70s, reclaiming its right to its own ancient heritage and sense of belonging.

And it was made very clear to the young Laird that *ha'oles* (outsiders without *ha*—the breath of life) were not welcome. Bullying was rife.

"I used to dream of coming back as a giant Hawaiian warrior—but then I'd wake up and I was still this skinny little blond kid."

—LAIRD HAMILTON

To be seen to "take on" the most powerful force—the sea—and seize the most venerated role—that of the surfer—may seem an obvious strategy to counteract the bullying.

But to do it required a staggering application of will—and a fierce refusal to submit to the given wisdom and pecking order.

Somewhere in Laird was a contrarian of tall order. A fighter waiting to be released. In doing what he did, he undertook a remarkable act of cultural disobedience. And asserted his unimpeachable islander credentials.

Disobedience is the true foundation of liberty—the obedient must be slaves.

—HENRY DAVID THOREAU,
CIVIL DISOBEDIENCE

Laird quotes Thoreau often. It is more than tossing out an easy sound-bite. And it is far more than just a way of downplaying the mammoth feat of self-assertion required of him to transgress the life he had. Disobedience is a rudder by which he has navigated his life, for better or worse. It has been a way of life. Since his earliest years, trouble was never far away. And the closer trouble got to Laird, the closer he got to the sea.

"It was a place I could escape to. I found equality in the sea. *The trouble was on the land.*"

—LAIRD HAMILTON

With the arrival of his new stepfather, Bill Hamilton, came more trouble.

The new "man of the house" was tough: sometimes a brutal disciplinarian. And he applied ever-increasing degrees of punishment to the tricky little boy, to contain his increasingly contrary nature.

But the disobedient child simply wore the strap-marks of his beatings as the scars of a valiant rebel warrior fighting the establishment.

But in conversing with Laird, it becomes obvious that his punk contrarian nature was potentially formed by more than just islander bullying and the beatings of his stepfather. Laird was, and is, more of a product of the culture he grew up in than even he might realize.

There is a belief that to be an islander is to always look "beyond" (unsurprisingly, one of Laird's favorite words). In her 2003 text on islanders and what shapes their identities, Marie-Louise Anderson pointed out:

Island boundaries invite transgression; inspire restlessness; demand to be breached; impel islanders "to explore and even to escape into the unknown."

—MARIE-LOUISE ANDERSON,
"NORFOLK ISLAND"

Laird's incessant need to look *beyond*, to transgress what's there, is the rocket fuel in his relentless innovation. He has a pathological need to keep turning over rocks and looking underneath. And his childlike curiosity seems to only increase with age.

> "He always did stuff that was a little bit 'not normal.' He had Velcro patches on his board, and he had boots with Velcro, and we're like, 'What the hell is that?' and then he took on the wave and he put his foot on the Velcro and he went—took off—he just went flying in the air, and we were all like, 'This guy's crazy.' He was always an innovator. He has something that just goes a little bit beyond."
>
> —TERRY CHUNG, LAIRD'S FRIEND AND FOILING PARTNER

With Laird, nothing is absolute. And failure breeds success.

His inability to "get down one wave, let alone get across it"—a failure in some people's eyes—simply raised the question "So, how *can* I?" The answer to this particular question was the innovation of foil boarding.

'Ohana

You will come across this word often in this book, in the thoughts, opinions, and explorations of both Laird and Gabby.

'Ohana is the Hawaiian word for family, the unit that sits at the very heart of all Hawaiian belief systems and social structures.

In Hawaiian culture all peoples are regarded as brothers and sisters, and all of them are bound by this collective sense of self, no matter how distant their association or relation.

'Ohana describes a family unit that extends far beyond blood relatives, to nonrelated people and immortals like a family god, or *'aumakua*.

'Ohana inspires a culture of shared responsibility and action—and a degree of social collaboration very particular to the Polynesian peoples.

It is the source of their pioneering spirit, and was central to their explorations across the Pacific:

> The *'ohana* (family) of old made it possible for the Polynesian voyagers to venture forth to unknown lands. This seafaring *'ohana* was able to travel thousands of miles on double-hulled canoes because it was in touch with nature and the gods. The *'ohana* felt safe because there were no barriers between the spiritual and cultural world. The Hawaiian was never separated from his makers and ancestors because the gods and demi-gods showed themselves everywhere; in the sky, in the earth, and in the sea.
>
> —CECILIA KAPUA LINDO,
> *THE SPIRIT OF 'OHANA AND THE POLYNESIAN VOYAGERS*

It is a system that is very much alive in the nature of the relationships Laird and Gabby make in the world.

Liferider intends to point to the spirit of *'ohana* as a dynamic and inextricable part of the network of collaboration and shared interest that Laird and Gabby create around themselves, and describe how it is central to the "contract of care" that they forge in initiatives such as XPT.

It intends to show how *'ohana* informs Laird's relentless innovation—and the spirit of the teams he builds around that innovation—as much as it contributes to his sense of connectivity to nature and feelings of responsibility to her.

> Cooperation comes largely from a notion of respect for one's own extended family (*'ohana*). And Hawaiians believe they have a genealogical connection as well as a spiritual connection to Mother Nature and all that she provides.
>
> —PHENG, MENG, KAUR, LEE, AND JEFFREY,
> *THE LIONHEARTS OF THE PACIFIC*

If there is one red thread from these conversations with both Laird and Gabby worth further and deeper exploration, it is *'ohana*—and the profound sense of connectivity it engenders, both between them and in the wider world.

The Power of Dreams

> "Make sure that your dreams are bigger than your memories."
>
> —LAIRD HAMILTON

This "Lairdism" is deceptively simple. Between the words and the letters of it lies everything you need to know about Laird in short order.

If you can be bothered to look beyond the obvious, a lot sits waiting for you.

Liferider seeks to explore the space between the Lairdisms and the YouTube clips—to "read between the lines" of Laird.

And, from the details and the nuances of what we find when we look a little deeper, *Liferider* looks to lay out a path for anyone with half an eye on riding life's wave.

The Five Pillars

To know what this book is, it is also quite helpful to know what it is not.

Liferider is not an exercise or personal fitness text, a practical guide to Laird's XPT course, or a reference book on his diet and regimes.

Liferider is not an extended lifestyle magazine piece on Laird's surf-and-sea existence or a dissertation on foil boarding.

Liferider is not a surf culture book.

Its intent is to cut much deeper into the substance of Laird and how he has mastered and managed his defiant warrior spirit to create rather than destroy a life for himself and his family.

Liferider is for everyone—from executives looking for inspiration and an understanding of the complexities of being human, and of how one might use those complexities to do extraordinary things, to someone living an ordinary landlocked life seeking to rebalance and reframe in some small way.

But if you need a bull's-eye, the clue is in Laird's age. He is an ageless fifty-four with a cold eye on enjoying fifty more years to the best of his ability. And in this book you'll find some clues to how anyone circling fifty might seek to do the same.

Liferider has five pillars—Death & Fear, Heart, Body, Soul, and Everything Is Connected—and it uses those pillars to take you on a journey from the science to the psyche of Laird, via the sea.

Liferider also has some action items in its flow. Things that allow any of us to start on our own journey toward nurturing our brilliant creature every day. Actions that we can all undertake, even when we're on our commute or at the office.

Liferider explores how the threads of Laird stitch together, how his worldview and life-practices combine to help him surf the wave of life, achieve what he has achieved, and still dream what he dreams.

Because dreams are universal. And we need to nurture as many of them as we can, now perhaps more than ever.

Barefoot Business

In this book you will also find reflective pieces on how each of the pillars plays out in Laird's business life.

There is much in lifestyle magazines at the moment on how entrepreneurs are increasingly seeking extreme sports and high-risk activities in search of clarity and balance in their lives. There would seem to be some value in reversing that analysis, by showing how an extreme athlete like Laird navigates the dry-land pressures and challenges of his entrepreneurial businesses.

And in a world where our understanding of the connections between the behaviors and actions of businesses—and their impact on our human and environmental well-being—grows stronger every day, Laird seems a good guy to ask.

The "Barefoot Business" sections explore how Laird and

Gabby partner to create, shape, and run the businesses they do, and how their philosophies lie at the heart of those businesses.

Honesty Is Everything

The contents of this book were developed over a succession of conversations with Laird, both in Malibu where he lives and shares XPT, and subsequently on Kauaʻi, his spiritual home.

In these conversations we explored each of the pillars through Laird's lens on life.

The tone of the book, as with everything else in it, is true to Laird.

Laird has one absolute rule he applies in life.

Raw honesty.

Always.

It is a rule he applies fiercely. Sometimes too fiercely for some. But it is his rule, and this book endeavors to honor it.

In that spirit, and apart from some tidying-up and light editing, what follows are Laird's raw words, occasionally supported by facts and information intended to illuminate the meaning, science, culture, or anthropology behind Laird's ideas.

DEATH & FEAR

When that shit comes down,
You just go to death.
That's honesty.
That's it.
You are an organism.
You are in competition with death.

—LAIRD HAMILTON

DEATH colors, shapes, illuminates, consumes, elevates, and inspires us.

Its turbulence; its randomness; the impenetrable veil around it; and its inevitable occurrence—these are what shape our material and spiritual nature. Who we are. What we are. Why we are.

But in many advanced Western cultures, we are losing our connection with death. We're pushing it away as an unwanted side effect of being human. A flaw in the organism. But in losing our connection to death, we lose something vital in life.

Here, Laird explores his relationship with death and with fear—and how the presence of death throughout his life has moved him, marked him, shaped his nature, and influenced how he chooses to live every moment. And he explores how fear can be a force for good in our lives, fuel for our fire—but only if we first seek to understand it, and then learn how to manage it.

LAIRD

You know, the ocean came and took people off the beach and you never saw them again. They weren't people that I was personally connected to, but I was exposed to people drowning and people getting brought up right in front of my house—bodies getting pulled in.

Death was a part of everyday life. It casts a shadow. Leaves its mark.

I had a friend—a guy who moved in next door to us—who I used to surf with quite a bit. I went to get him one morning and he was laying on the floor of his house, dead. He didn't come out as he always did, so I went in to look for him and I found him lying there.

I've been exposed to a fair amount of death from a young age. Situations where I would come across people being dead, either through drowning or natural causes. Those situations were probably more than a normal boy might experience.

The majority of the death I was exposed to was ocean-related. People just getting sucked away and never being seen again; or floating in five days later. You get an instinct for it.

I remember once being down at the beach and just feeling that something wasn't right. Wasn't good. You get to know the water. To sense things. So there I am, pretty young, telling a guy not to go in the water—and the guy telling me to "piss off." He then goes in the water, and the guy drowns—and then his son drowns.

I think that situation affected me deeply. It changed me. It made me a lot more aggressive. Once I could tell that someone shouldn't be going in the water; that they didn't have the experience, the knowledge, to be there; I'd walk up and tell them.

I could be ten years old and go in there and swim all day, and I'd see adults go in there and drown. So at a certain point I really started getting in people's faces, and telling them that they really shouldn't be going out there. It didn't matter to me that I was just a kid.

I mean, no one likes being told what to do, right? Especially by some punky kid. They're kind of like, "You don't tell me what to do."

But it's the sea. You have to accept it. You have got to go to it with respect in your heart.

"Laird wasn't really disobedient—he was still practicing his intelligence; he was putting other people to the test; although they thought they were testing him, he was testing everybody else."

—COPPIN COLBURN, HAMILTON FAMILY FRIEND

Surfing was dangerous even when I was small. I lived at the Pipeline and they were pulling guys in with skulls cracked open, faces smashed—guys that were tough. Surfers got hurt a lot at that beach because that's a very dangerous beach, and then I went from that to moving to another island where a couple of the beaches that I played on were equally dangerous. One of my favorites, Lumahai, was the second deadliest beach in the state of Hawaii. It ate three or four people every year—sometimes more. So I played and lived in places where people got smashed up a lot. Died. A lot.

A lot of people get hurt in surfing. Sometimes it's just minor stuff. Stitches and puncture wounds. And sometimes because of the nature of that sport, you'd get smashed heads, broken necks—something heavier. And people's skill was everything in surviving in that water. The equipment they were riding wasn't nearly as reliable.

But even so, there's a forgiveness about the ocean in one way. A lot more people should be getting a lot more hurt a lot more often than they do, given what they're doing. It's remarkable that the Pipeline doesn't take more lives.

So in the world I grew up in, death and your relationship with the ocean are one.

I think there's a through line that exists among all people who are connected to the ocean. There's always one or two random hot rods out there, but for most people attached to the sea, there's a certain respect that you have for the ocean, and a pretty conscious awareness because of the nature of the environment itself.

The environment is so powerful that you're going to have death on your mind somewhere. And you're going to believe in something greater. I don't think there's a lot of atheists in the lineup, just given the nature of the magic and the beauty and the intricacy of what the ocean is.

A friend of mine calls the ocean "the soup of life." It's a pretty complex and very alive organism. And it doesn't discriminate. It will just pound you.

And in that moment—in that turbulence, when you lose the edges of what you know in that white-water tumble dryer—that's where science meets the spiritual. If you're underwater, you can't breathe. It doesn't matter who you are and what you can do, pretty much we're all the same guys sooner or later under the water. We all have the innate fear of drowning. We all have the presence to understand that there's no oxygen below the waterline; and there's big creatures that live there and heavy stuff happens.

"Nobody knows that ocean better than Laird; ever since he was a little kid, he belonged there in the water. The ocean communicates to him. And he knew that—something about that water that drew him to the ocean—if he could sleep in the ocean, he would sleep in the ocean. He respected it and knew it—and he knows the ocean can take his life at any time."

—COPPIN COLBURN

My description of riding a wave is simple: there's no beginning and no end—it's just a continuation. Where you start and where you left off are just phases or moments on the same line—on the same continuum. And that's life, too.

Death has always been there for me, I suppose. And not always just the kind served by the sea. Not knowing my real dad—that's a kind of death. Is it a physical death? No—but there's grief there, for sure.

If I look back on my father's absence—I think that's what death ultimately is—they're gone—they're absent. For me, I think the initial exposure to the concept of someone being dead was ultimately the fact that I didn't have a dad. My dad was gone, whether he was alive or not—I didn't even know. He wasn't there—ever—on the phone or in a letter—there was nothing.

I realize now that I was grieving that absence and loss. I just started from the beginning of my life with that concept of someone being gone.

That was a version of death that I was experiencing at a very young age. I think that definitely has to be the beginning of the foundation of my perspective on death.

Death comes in many forms, and some of it really gets to you. It shapes you. It opens your eyes. And you see how it makes every second of life precious.

Polynesians are not terrified or overpowered by the phenomena of the dead. Inborn talent, trained sensitivity, and education enable them to handle phenomena as naturally as they do the winds and the waves.

JOHN P. CHARLOT, *POLYNESIAN RELIGIONS*

My friend who I used to surf with as a kid was diagnosed with terminal cancer. They told him he had six months to live, so he just moved in where we lived and went surfing every day and he ended up living eight years longer. I spent a lot of time with him.

And he had the presence of death around him. He lived with death. *I got no time, I got no time.*

I think that definitely had an influence on me—in the way I wanted to live my life. To make sure that I was always living in the present. *How would we live if we knew that we were going to go tomorrow?* We don't think about that enough now. It would be nice to cultivate that feeling more often, and really think about how you would live if you knew tomorrow was the last day.

I had a friend, Bunker. He was my buddy. He overdosed and died. I spent a lot of time with him when he was a kid. I watched him just transform from a happy person to an unhappy person. I couldn't help him. I was too young and he was too crazy, but I felt like somebody killed him. I feel like he got killed by people that were trying to take advantage of his wealth. That affected me a lot.

When somebody lives for the ocean, they're on it, in it, and then they go and get drowned. That's one thing. But when you have got a fatal condition, a terminal cancer or illness of some kind, and you're just dangling, waiting for the thing to drop, those are two different things right there. When you live under the truth of "Hey, I have some sickness and I'm going to die—I'm going to die in the next day or two or month"—when you have that hanging over you, that definitely influences your behavior—versus when you're young and you think you're invincible!

Let's be clear here. Death is part of life. It's the cycle. Where I grew up it was pretty ordinary in some ways.

Death is just part of the deal.

It's no surprise to me that when you look at many high-performing people in any field, they will have the echo or the evidence of some high-stress point, some emotional trauma, on them; something that stressed the organism. Abandonment. Poverty. Abuse. Humiliation. Grief. Loss.

I suppose in that way death has often been a relentless stress point on me. And in a weird way perhaps it has evolved me in particular ways.

My mom's death had big effect on me. I'm only just starting to realize how much.

But one thing about her preparation for death was that it didn't put a burden on me. I didn't have any potential resentments that could come from somebody you care for dying and leaving a big mess, and then you have to go clean it all up. That wasn't the case—if anything, it was the opposite. You learn from that.

I was in good standing with my mom, so I was lucky. She and I had just recently reconciled our differences, so we were pretty OK. I think that helped me—going through the mourning of it—because we were good. There was no regret. Nothing lost to us. Regret is a killer. That stuff will tear you up.

I found equality in the sea.
It was a place I could escape to.
There was something there I needed.
The trouble was on the land.

—LAIRD HAMILTON

Sure, in my need for the ocean, I may have been running away from stuff. But I was also running towards stuff.

Let's not forget, the sea was really exciting. Super thrilling. You would come back and feel invigorated, feeling so alive.

The sea is thorough: all-consuming—literally. You go into it and you're immersed—physically, emotionally, spiritually—separated from any of the things that you're thinking about—or that you don't want to think about.

My need to connect with the ocean is ever present. I

naturally gravitate towards the power of it because it's the most honest and the most productive way to live for me.

Life is here. Death is here. They're both of each other—as close to each other as the negative and the positive of a battery—intertwined.

That's why you see people doing things that seem to be so dangerous—because that's where you feel the most alive. Hanging in that space between life and death. Of course we're going to go there: that just makes complete sense to me. If you make it so nothing's dangerous and there is no risk—then how does the living feel? Pretty boring. You need one to offset the other. Pleasure doesn't really have the power it does without pain. The nature of pleasure is directly related to the experience of pain—that discomfort of the senses. Those things are interrelated. They need each other to exist. We need fear to exist completely; to know what calm is. What serenity is.

But let's be clear. Feeling fear and being scared are two very different things. Fear is about respect. Fear leads to informed action. How we manage and control fear is an elementary part of survival. Fear reminds us that we need to continuously assess risk. That's honesty. That's respect for things bigger and stronger than you.

"He's always waiting. I can feel it; some days I feel for him. I used to dream that I could produce big waves for Laird—I used to have dreams that would say, 'OK. Here's the deal,' like a power; 'It's gonna come tomorrow and it's gonna be twenty feet tall.' I used to wish that for him because sometimes it's a long time.

"And he has a fear—a fear of a flat planet. For him

LAIRD

it's maybe the only time he can take all his skills and put them to the test, but also be completely consumed in it."

—GABBY REECE

Fear is about being on. Fear is about awareness. Where does that ability to switch "on" come from, to manage it? It can come from lots of places. For me there was a tipping point in my relationship with fear: the first time I can remember switching that awareness "on."

When I was a kid in Hawaii there was always something in the air. The threat was present. In front of my house, around my house, at school. There was no one particular bully, but there were always fights. That's kids. That's boys. But it was beyond that. There was something—a general threat. I was aware of it, and I needed to be. I'd sit at the back of the class, or in the back of a restaurant, always on, super aware. *Who's that? Who are they?* From a very young age I needed to be "on."

"He was just a little kid. I think he was like twelve years old or ten years old—this peaky *ha'ole* kid. We weren't mean or anything, we were just 'you know where you stand.'

"We just threw him off the bridge, and he fell in the water and he swam to the side—and then he just gathered all these rocks and then we all ran away because he was throwing the rocks at us. And after that he totally forgot about it. That's Laird."

—TERRY CHUNG

When we first arrived on the island, I was five or six years old, and my mom and I were invited to a luau—a big family party with a kalua pig roast. There were these kids. They were bigger than me and older than me. And they said, "Hey, come play with us." And they took me to the top of this mountain, and then they just ran away and I didn't know where the hell I was. And it was getting dark and I was utterly lost. I remember I was really scared. I'd never been scared like that. I started coming down the hill and I could hear them laughing. I couldn't see them but I could hear them.

Eventually I got to the bottom, and between the hill and the ocean was a road. And I got back down to the road, and they were all lined up on the road.

The luau was behind them. And they're there. And I'm scared.

Then I just put my head down and I just ran straight at them. And they just opened up. That was a tipping point. That was their way of saying, "Hey, welcome to town. Welcome to the valley. Welcome to our world."

So from that moment I saw the way things were. From that moment I'm "on." From that moment I am processing fear. And I'm picking a fight with it.

I started to gravitate towards bigger boys. I would do crazy stuff that no one would do. I wanted to be friends with these older guys, so they'd make me do all kinds of radical stuff. "If you want to be our friend and hang out with us, you've got to jump this jump with this bike."

"At a very young age Laird did something that takes most of us a lifetime to do, and that is to identify who he is. And once you identify who you are, you just run with it.

"He knew who he was when he was a little young boy. He's perfected that because he's been working at it for a lifetime."

—COPPIN COLBURN

To assess fear properly, you need to know what you're looking at. And as humans we have some things that can cloud that judgment.

I tell my girls, your imagination's always greater than reality—you imagine things to be much worse than they are.

Our imagination messes with us. Our imagination and its storytelling abilities—something which makes us different from every other animal—our imagination which can create these stories that we can all believe in, is the same imagination which gives us the ability to make things much bigger and crazier than they really are. The longer you wait on the top of the cliff, the harder it is to jump off—because your imagination goes to work.

Every irrational fear that I had entertained in past voyages had now been realized, and yet now that the worst had happened I found myself unafraid and completely calm.

—PETER WADHAMS, *A FAREWELL TO ICE*

There are times, though, when you don't need an imagination to make something scary. The cold hard truth of it is scary enough.

The scariest moment in my life was being lost at sea—between the islands. I was paddling on my board, in heavy fog. I lost the horizon. I lost my bearings. Sixty miles north of the Big Island.

A coast guard helicopter finally pulled me out. But that was after twenty-four hours in which to do a lot of thinking. You get to do a lot of thinking and feeling in that moment. About how I'd die. About how I'd lived. About the people I love. About what I'd do if I was rescued. How I'd change. What I would change.

Did it stop me pushing it? Taking risks? Embracing fear? No. But it certainly rounded off some of the corners.

The majority of society is usually living vicariously through the risk-takers, whether the risk-takers are the hunters, or the warriors, or some guy on a board or in a wingsuit. Most people don't want to go dance with the wolves, they don't want to be on that edge—but they can appreciate that it must enhance the sensation and the pleasures of living. We innately know that, which is why we're attracted to watching it. It's entertainment.

We're really under no threat at all for most of our lives; when we sit there strapped into some VR thing, or on a game platform, however crazy the ride is, we're only getting half of the experience. Even when we're stressing the body and mind in pool training—there is no risk. Even if you find ways to put yourself into "risky" situations—create stress for yourself—you're not putting yourself in a true position of risk, one where true threat exists, so you're not going to get the rewards of that.

Risk is something I feel. It's sensory. It's fear. It heightens everything. A big part of the experience is the feeling of it. I can feel the intensity.

There's a sensation that comes from being "on." When I'm finished I realize that sensation is part of the thing I was looking for. I went there to get that feeling. So I think sometimes it's less about the wave and more about that feeling.

The hair stands up on my neck; smell, touch, hearing, everything becomes heightened—a hyperawareness. This is what creates the sense of everything slowing down. I am in a state of heightened awareness, so I'm bringing in information at a super-high level. It's a combination of adrenaline-induced heart rate, respiratory acceleration, visual enhancement. I recognize the situation; I know what's going on. Especially when a wave comes down on me and I'm dragging the bottom. There's no horizon. That's a big part of it too. It creates a deeper immersion into the moment.

Is that a crazy position to put yourself in? Maybe. But we do what we do. And for some of us that feeling is the reason for doing it. Maybe we're just redirecting stuff. Or maybe we're just getting off on the "on."

We can rely on the organism to deliver that feeling. Risky and dangerous situations will switch us on without us asking. That's the organism going to work, unconsciously or otherwise. Suddenly we're at the edges of ourselves.

Stand on the edge of a cliff on a kite or in a wingsuit, and you put yourself into a heightened and highly vulnerable state. You are going to need all of your faculties. And when the fight-or-flight thing kicks in, it's the organism doing what it's programmed to do. This is a system built over millions of years. You need to trust it and listen to it. And keep listening to it.

If you do what I do, the danger comes from the complacency of doing fear-inducing stuff again and again. Your organism gets used to it. Complacency from success is dangerous. The minute you think, *Oh I've been here before, I know how this rolls*, it becomes dangerous. Hang on to the original feeling of fear. Don't try and scrub it away.

The organism is designed with this fight-or-flight system. It's a highly efficient and effective system proven over millions of years. It knows what to do in the moment, and it knows what to do with the by-products of it. All that adrenaline. All that CO_2. All the by-products of that moment.

Now, that's fine on a wave or three thousand feet up in the air. Because your system is going through the whole process: the cycle of heightening and then winding down. You complete the cycle.

But a lot of stress can be toxic in everyday life. If turned on itself, the system that is designed to keep us alive can become the source of the wrong kind of stress.

Just walking down the street, or in a meeting, something kicks off the organism's defense mechanism—some kind of threat—and the organism goes into overdrive, and suddenly you've got a lot of powerful reactions running in you. Your fight-or-flight mechanism goes to full alert and the adrenaline is pumping, heart rate's up, your muscles tense up, you start drawing in more oxygen. All that needs somewhere to go—to do what it was designed to do.

If it has nowhere to go, then the system gets overloaded and that's not good.

In everyday life, we're not that good at shaking off

moments of high stress and all of the side effects and by-products that come from that. A lot of people are self-inducing overload through unmanaged stress. It's become an indulgence—something we allow to happen. It's not like you actually fight or take flight and utilize that surge of cranked-up energy and awareness in you. Most of the time, if you're getting cranked all the time and holding on to it, the body experiences a degree of toxicity just trying to absorb it all and process it.

If a car speeds over the crossing and almost hits you and you react, that's the organism, the fight-or-flight system kicking in. But you can't just keep indulging that, cussing and reliving it all day. You have to let it go. By hanging on to the moment, you keep yourself in that state, and the system keeps producing the chemical reactions to deal with it. And that's inefficient and toxic. As an organism we're not designed to do that.

It doesn't help that most of us are not living well. That just makes it worse. We're not sleeping well; we don't eat properly. Too much screen time. Dysfunctional social lives.

We've all been there. There was a time when I didn't take good care of myself. I wasn't as prudent with my overall fitness.

The problem is that it's even harder for the system to process these fight-or-flight moments when it's underperforming. A healthy organism can process a massive amount of this type of stress. But most of us are far from pure health.

And we tend towards the no-brainer solution. It's a human thing. I like to think that because we're mostly water, like water we look for the path of least resistance. The easiest option. The no-brainer.

Drink. There's an answer to all that leftover adrenaline.

Especially when you're jagged. I've been on the wrong side of that stuff.

And we're all so wrapped up in stuff that we can't see it. Realization is not always instantaneous. Sometimes it reveals itself. Gabby and I were at odds, having difficulties in our relationship. And it took a while for me to realize. It took me a while to see that there was a pattern.

After a long day on the water—big water—I've been smashed by a wave a few times, I'm in a super-heightened state of almost post-traumatic stress. And suddenly that bottle of Bordeaux looks pretty attractive. That looks like it'll do it.

But it doesn't work. I became unkind, shitty with the people closest to me.

When we mix that toxic soup inside us with a load of extra poisons—drink, drugs, whatever—it's self-destructive.

That's what unprocessed fear does to us. That's what happens when we don't either manage the fear process from the get-go or scrub it down properly beyond the moment. We get junked up on the wrong kind of stress. We get overwhelmed with negative stuff. And then just make it worse with some quick fix. You have to nurture your way out of there.

Fear is a powerful tool for the organism. But you've got to know what to do with it.

And awareness of that is half the solution. Just recognizing that that is what you're doing is half the battle. Just realizing that there is a cause and effect at work.

But not everyone has the fortitude to deal with stress head-on. It's too raw. That's where immersion can play a role. Indirect ways of counseling the organism. Rerouting the stress through immersion in something.

That's where things like meditation, or mechanical mantras like sailing, surfing, running, or climbing come in and can play a powerful role in redirecting the stress. Because they force you into the moment. They consume you and reroute the negative stuff.

To really live, to really be out there, you need to have figured out how to process stress. Otherwise you're just drowning in it. It consumes you in all the wrong ways.

And you have to pay attention to every spoke in the wheel. Not just the source or nature of the stress itself. Sleep. Hydration. Relationships, everything matters. If my relationship with my wife isn't OK or if my kids aren't OK, then I can't be out there. I'm trapped.

The whole organism needs to be tended to. The closer you are to tending to the complete organism, the better you can process this stuff. Life needs that level of attention.

We have to make life productive. Make it a good run. Make it something that you can enjoy while you do it. And that takes a little risk. Risk-takers, I mean *big* risk-takers, might push that a lot. But this isn't just extreme sports stuff. We all have to take some risks out there in the world sometimes, and we have to trust that that's a good thing. And not just feel like we need to not bother, or just give up because we hit an age or did a thing that says, "I'm done."

When people talk about retiring, they go, "I'm going to work my whole life. I'm going to get a bunch of money and I'm going to retire."

And that's cool. It's a decision. And you stick to it. But the danger is that in just trying to survive and thrive while you're doing it, to hit that mark, you miss a lot of living. And that can create regret.

The danger is that by the time you get to a point where

you can retire, you're going to be so exhausted—you're not even going to be able to enjoy your retirement. So you may as well try and live a little more along the way.

You don't know what's going to happen. You should live that life. Try and live in the moment. Fear the unknown, but don't be scared of it.

Do we have to plan for what might be ahead? Sure; I think that's part of it. But somewhere between what is and what might be, that's the dance, right there. That's where we need to exist. You can live like there's no tomorrow, while still being a little bit prepared when tomorrow comes.

That's part of the art. To live in the Now but make sure that you're faced in the right direction—so you're not caught off-guard when you wake up the next day. Your continual evolution as an organism in the Now will, in a way, prepare you for tomorrow—that will be your preparation for everything to come.

But all of this ultimately comes down to one thing: being clear about your purpose in life. Your purpose in doing what you do. Our relationship with death. When you're taking risks. If you're out there shaking the tree. Be clear on the Why.

I use big wave riding as an example. When you get yourself in a situation where you're tested, it always goes back to why you're there. If in the moment, in the middle of the test, beware if you can't answer the question "Why am I here?" In the moment of truth when that shit's coming down, when you ask yourself why you're here, your answer will determine if you're still here a few moments later.

Your "why" is everything. If it's your core, your essence— if it's everything you know—then keep going. If it's anything else, if it's material or ego-driven, at some point your instinct is going to desert you. You're going to freak out. You will have that "get me out of here" moment. And that's bad. In a high-risk situation, that's failure right there.

But if you're following your intuition and you're following your heart—then you may think, *I don't know if I'm ready for the ass whipping I'm going to get—but I'm here and I know why I'm here.*

As for what happens when I'm *not* here—that's a conversation. There's a whole lot of versions of that. That's where science and religion dance. Living between the known and the unknown. Doesn't matter how great you think you are, or what others say about you. You've got to have the humility to accept that we don't know everything and maybe we never will.

"If you want anyone's respect in Hawaii, you've got to have humility. I could take LeBron James or Ronaldo or whoever you want to say, and Laird probably does the heaviest thing by far—and is by far the most humble."

—GABBY REECE

Perhaps you don't get to know what happens when you die, because maybe it would affect how you live, and you need to learn how to live by what you see and what you hear now.

You don't get the luxury of having this other piece of information that could affect the way that you do everything. To have it would mean that you wouldn't be truly experiencing what's happening here. You wouldn't get all the rewards of those lessons. It would stop people from trying to live to the best of their abilities.

I think at a certain point the spiritual side naturally overrides us because we don't have the data. Sure, we have the biological information or the medical science to know what happens to us physically when we die, but in regards to our conscious self and what happens to that, we have no science to explain it. But we *feel* it. There's something. I know it, instinctually. I'm clear that there is something greater than us; greater than me—far beyond what I can comprehend. I don't know what that looks like exactly, but I will continue to believe that there's something—because there's no science that says there's not.

Unknowing is part of us and how we evolve. The spiritual part carries us past our limitations—past the limitations of what we know.

"Accepting and undertaking risk is how we evolved as a species. Just because we have evolved beyond needing to take this level of risk in our everyday lives doesn't mean that those in-built competencies just disappear."

—LAIRD HAMILTON

It's the same with risk. People wouldn't do the impossible. People wouldn't take themselves to new limits if they worked within, or accepted, the given. In the early days of the car, people thought we'd die if we went over twenty miles an hour. Not-knowing is a charge. It makes us wonder. It makes us curious to know what's on the other side—what's beyond it?

Perhaps as an organism we evolve because we don't have all the answers. We keep reaching.

I believe it's complicated enough to just try to live true to yourself—to what's written in your heart—and to live true to this space and this time. That's a pretty tough job, and to be trying to seek out the meaning of everything won't really change what you have to do and what you have to go through.

BAREFOOT BUSINESS

Fear, failure, & riding the risk

Failure—and the fear of it—is one of the greatest barriers to starting and growing businesses.

Riding risk is the banal, everyday truth of everyone who has ever started or run a business.

The entrepreneur's responses to risk, and the likelihood of fear or massive failure at both the emotional and rational levels, will color, shape, and define the degrees of their success.

They can predict the entrepreneur's ability to manage the turbulence that comes with building and leading businesses.

The fear of a massive failure in business—bankruptcy, for example, and the loss of status and identity that comes with it—is something that the resilient entrepreneur must always entertain.

Cultures and sectors that embrace the spirit of failure and see it as a positive force move more quickly to solutions, breakthroughs, and repair in the event of turbulence and volatility.

Here, Laird and Gabby explore the subject of risk-taking and its personal impact and effect in their professional lives.

LAIRD

Risk-taking in business is table stakes. And risk comes in many forms.

But given what I do on the water, risk in business is very, very different in how it demonstrates itself and how I feel about it.

I think risk has a certain formula to it—a certain logic.

If you're not prepared to get the biggest wave of the day on your head, then you probably shouldn't be out there. Business is no different; just the outcome's a little less severe.

I quote Don Wildman all the time: *"This isn't life or death."*

These risks you take in business aren't life or death. They aren't critical. And if you're not willing to take a certain amount of risk, then you aren't going to have the opportunity to experience the maximum success.

It's part of the deal: no risk, no reward. And the greater the risk, the more the reward, but it doesn't mean that you're not fearful of failure—but I think that when you've failed enough times and you've been through that, it has less impact on you.

You know by then that you can always start again, so I think you have to have faith, which means that you believe in the possibility of success.

You have to believe in the possibility of success more than the probability of failure.

Because if you don't, then you're just going to be scared of doing anything. If you don't think there's a possibility for success in what you're doing, in the business you're starting or running, then every little thing you do is going to make you scared.

But this is not life or death. This is not risk-taking at the extremity of the organism.

If business people want that, they go put on a kite suit, or go BASE jump.

They experience the real sensation of being alive, of the risk.

People can make their business their greatest risk— that's their thing. But I think that's just replacing the fact that they really don't have another place where that extremity of emotion can get exercised.

If you want your business to be your wave, that's fine. But before long, if risk—going to the edges of yourself and your capabilities—is your thing, you're going to go looking for the real version.

I think any one of my businesses failing wouldn't feel great. Right now my superfoods business is the most successful, with the potential for the most growth—so that would be the one that would be the most disappointing if it failed.

But I'm not defined by the success or failure of any of my businesses. They are important to me, but they are not who I am or what I've done.

If your business is your whole identity, I think you may have problems waiting there.

I think that when you hang the whole thing, your whole self, on that business, you put an added extra pressure into the situation that I think would only inhibit its success.

It needs to be important, don't get me wrong. You need to make things meaningful. But is it defining you as a person—the success or the failure? Because that introduces the potential for desperation.

When your whole self is totally reliant on the success or failure of your business, and something starts to go wrong, you're not going to have the clarity you need to make the right decision. You're going to get desperate. And if you deal from a position of desperation, it's always bad—it's always a bad spot to be in, in anything in life.

It puts you in a position where you cannot operate at your full potential. You become encumbered by all the ifs and the what-ifs, and that's easy to do. You put that stuff on yourself, and then all of a sudden you're like a self-fulfilling prophecy.

It kills your confidence, which kills your creativity; your ability to think smart.

You become more conservative.

You see young companies where their success is really based on their risk-taking—and then, as soon as they get successful, they go into conservative mode. All their energy is suddenly channeled into protecting the identity they have, what they've accrued—and that's where the business plateaus. The business always plateaus when they get conservative.

An athlete can do that, too. When you're younger, you're taking risks, willing to do everything, sucking up the failures, getting back on it, and then, soon as you get successful, all of a sudden you don't want to take as many risks anymore.

I think it's easy to fall into that trap, because it's a human condition that once you reach a certain level of provision—once you're providing for yourself—then you move into protection mode, a completely different mode to the one that made you successful.

And that means you become disconnected from yourself—the authentic thing that made what you built happen. There's maximum risk in that disconnection.

My businesses are all connected to my brand—they are part of me. The image is always connected, so there's always continuity amongst those things.

But at the same time, I like a certain separation—because it's like building five fires. If one's really starting to take, you just add wood and get it going; and ones that aren't burning so well, you just don't give as much energy to those.

But they all have a certain role—there's a continuity amongst all of them that is reflective of what your corporate philosophy is.

I think the corporate philosophy is pretty consistent across all of our businesses.

Whether it's a business you're starting on, or a product you're developing, there has to be consistency in the image—how the image is portrayed.

I don't think that fundamentally changes, no matter how different the product or the business. You may adjust aspects of it for a specific product, but in general your philosophy, and your image, has to be pretty well controlled.

You have to protect it—because that's the only unambiguous visible value. And that value has to be protected, and also the message has to be consistent, because otherwise it's confusing. As long as all of your enterprises are authentic, then it's a lot easier, because if you only tell one "truth" you don't have to keep trying to remember what you said as you move across them.

The relationship between them is important. They feed off each other.

When you fix a North Star there's no confusion, and people can start to identify with your brand philosophy—so consistent messaging is going to help. If you have a consistent message, then you're going to be able to cross-pollinate easier.

People want to know there's a consistent message in things; so the people that you're working with will be more motivated and less chaotic, because you're not creating confusion around what you're promoting. Confusion can be dangerous.

Confusion creates uncertainty. And it can create identity issues.

And sometimes that is as likely to come from overcontrolling something as it will from just allowing everything to be chaos.

When you plug in a formula—you can lose your personality, your identity. It's all about staying unique, it's always about being unique—unique is everything right?

That's nature's rule. The system is the system, but within it everything is different.

Every snowflake is different—that's the nature of everything—that's foundational. Every leaf is a leaf, but every leaf on every plant is different.

Risk can also lie in being overcompetitive. You can kill yourself stone-dead by overreaching your limitations.

If you're overcompetitive, that really limits your possibility. If you're confident, you'll naturally find your level. But if you're trying to overprotect and overengineer, that's a sign of insecurity—and that's a limitation that's going to hold back your potential. You're just holding your breath.

If you are open, then it's like the law of the universe—you can embrace the ebb and the flow. That'll be the natural energy of your business or your idea.

Survival is about adaptation. The ability to ebb and flow, to breathe in and breathe out with a business idea, is a huge part of managing risk and exposure.

When I relate that to the ocean, and adapting in the water, first of all: every wave is different—which will create some new circumstance. So you must be able to adapt, quickly. They say the best-laid plans are the ones most easily changed.

Everything is an opportunity for improvement—that's the interesting part.

Once it's all routed in—that's less interesting. I think that becomes less interesting. That's the point at which you have to let it go. It's time to hand it over to someone who is better built for routing, scaling, and control.

Once you understand what it takes to be a successful business, success itself can become a formula. There's a certain approach or nature to your success that you can start to implement into the other businesses. It needs to vary with different products, but you can look at certain sectors and you can start to map how your nature of success might play in them.

You know that there will be certain needs and requirements to deliver a business. You'll need this and that—reoccurring revenue, multiple distribution points, whatever it takes, and then, once you've put those together, you've got a business. But have you got a success?

Sometimes, for all your planning, it just doesn't fit the success formula you've shaped. And you have to decide whether that's something worth your energy.

Making decisions on what business to start and tend to has a lot to do with what you choose to call success. There might be another reason for you to be in business—another reason to be doing it. At a certain point, it might not be for the success of a business in commercial terms. It might be because you need something else that the business is providing you.

When I think about the board and equipment business—it's a tough business. They're expensive items. People buy one and then they don't buy another for years.

But I need equipment. And I'd rather be riding my own boards than someone else's. So even if the board business doesn't have a lot of margin in it, and isn't super successful, it provides an important spoke in my wheel.

If the business can somewhat subsidize itself and provide me with what I need, it's better than me using a lesser product. Whatever happens, indirectly or directly, it is still going to benefit my other businesses. It expands my brand and my creative fulfillment.

The nature of the success of a business will determine your creative fulfillment, and there's something to be said about those things providing a platform to continue to promote the brand in different venues.

So there are businesses of mine, like boards, where there's an opportunity to make it commercially successful—but that won't dictate whether I continue or not.

And the possibility for success is genuine—but you're not hanging on that cliff of whether it is going to make you or break you.

If you're running several businesses, no single business should be able to make or break you. Each one should be able to make you, or at least make meaningful contributions to your success, but the failure of one shouldn't bring down everything.

GABBY

I think Laird has come close enough to the feeling that he might die that his sense of what's threatening is just different. Does he worry about failure? I don't think so.

Remember, being the novice, being the beginner, is a comfortable place for Laird. Being a beginner involves failure. And that tests him. Business is no different.

His stand-up business has never really thrived, but it's weird because Laird's greatest connection to the most people will be stand-up paddling—because they will have been able to do it. They're not going to foil, they're not going to ride giant waves—they're going to stand-up paddle on a river or on a lake; maybe by the sea. So it's the way he could best connect to the most people, and it never really did much.

It sometimes takes only the smallest thing to inspire a business. Sometimes just an observation.

Paul Hodge, the cofounder of Laird Superfood, would watch people coming in and asking Laird to make them coffee, year after year, and literally, one day, said, "How hard can this be?" And then, in three months, we had samples and the beginning of the Coffee Creamer business.

And the way the business has grown I think has genuinely excited Laird, as much as that can excite Laird. He gets real passionate about figuring this stuff out—the balance; the ingredients and how they come together. Coffee plays a big role in his fuel-up regime. He doesn't do the espresso black, super-jacked caffeine thing. He needs slow release. And the Creamer is the delivery system that feeds the energy out evenly. So this isn't just a Laird-branded product. This is way more.

If that business were to fail, I think for him that really would be disappointing.

But those are decisions that always come up in business. *Is it failing? Why? And what can we do about it?*

Sometimes you have to be the one that calls it.

So you're vigilant. You're going to look at the landscape of your businesses. Which is the one that needs care? You're just looking at it realistically, and you're just looking at the economics. You're looking at the market. You're looking at the team. You're looking at the evaluations. You're looking at the sales. You're looking at all of it. And you go, "OK, at the moment, looking at the entire universe, this one isn't cutting it."

It's not something that you can actually always control.

I've been doing this long enough where I look at it and go, "That's out of my control."

Those are the things that you can't explain. So I think when you talk about business, you do the best you can, and you try to really look ahead and be intelligent, and keep checking back in to your heart source and why you're doing it.

And making sure that you're really clear. And that you know that when you just say, "I'll ride it," you're not going to pretend you were planning it that way. Whatever comes; it's like, "Yep, that is part of business, that is part of entrepreneurship."

There will be times when you think, *We did everything right and it didn't work, and we kind of did a third of the stuff pretty well, and then something just happened—like some weird magic moment—and it stopped working.*

So I think that's an important thing to understand: stuff doesn't always work; however, you had to try.

We've done other things that haven't worked—and so

that's part of it too. You can't think, *I'm going to go and swing and hit the fences every time.*

I've spent lots of money personally on ideas and things where I was trying to pull the pieces together and it was not the right time and it didn't work, so you waste a lot of money. I've been down that path. It goes with the territory.

What happens is you learn first of all how to cut the line quick when you understand that one or two of the things are not right. And that's all it takes.

You have to think, *We've come halfway—so do I go the distance? Or do I turn around?*

It's also understanding who to be around. Initially you want to be around really smart people, but then you realize you really need to be around really *collaborative* people.

And they aren't always pleasant. Occasionally we have to swim with the sharks.

With entrepreneurship, I believe that people are afraid to try because it's overwhelming, and it takes a long time.

You've got to have some stamina and belief. That's where you're talking about your original intention and your ideas of doing something. If you can always be connected to those, they will carry you through. Those always resonate with you. And they need to—because it takes a long time. It takes years and years. It always takes longer than you think.

The good news is: you don't live and die in the making of a business. But when a business or an idea does falter or die, you don't just cut and run.

Or perhaps that's just me. People seem to run from what they see as failure. But you need to finish it. It's like Laird and the wave—you've got to finish the ride, whatever happens.

So you close it out. Out of respect for the people who

invested time or money in it. Because I'm looking at the long term—the investment in the relationship.

I think that's another big part of it: always standing by the decisions you've made and being accountable for your part in it. Doing the extra, going over everything—going "beyond" every single time.

So if you do have to drop the guillotine, it's comfortable, and you can also see those people and be OK with it—that's the thing.

You've got to be OK with that stuff. That's being responsible to the people you do business with, and accepting what comes with that. That's good karma.

Keep It Real

How we experience and process the fundaments of death and fear is critical to how we successfully navigate life. They have shaped us at a genetic, physical, emotional, and philosophical level over hundreds of thousands of generations. Regardless of our best efforts to put them in a box or hide away from them, they remain ever present, sitting just beneath the shiny foil of our scratch-card existence; unavoidable and immutable. Scratch the foil and, at some point, we will find them staring back at us.

The embrace and celebration of death and fear are arts that we are losing to history and myth. It's as if we feel that we have evolved beyond them.

But this is a lie that allows us to luxuriate in an illusion: that death is negotiable. But death is *not* negotiable for us. And a complete absence of fear is evidence of an evolutionary dislocation that will neither benefit nor improve us.

The simple truth is that, to be complete, to be real—and to exist in the reality of our Now—we need both fear and death alive within us.

As he makes very clear, the contract between Laird and life is predicated on the fact that it will end. He believes that, while our tenure in this life might be defined to a great degree by the fitness of the organism we are, death is inevitable. And that it is in the tension between life and death—that friction—that we find ourselves truly alive.

"We are in competition with death."

In this simple acceptance lies his greatest strength. No illusion of immortality or delusion of negotiated being. Not even a whiff of the age-defying vanities we seem increasingly consumed by.

The presence of death and fear certainly keeps Laird true to the existence he has, and to the person he needs to be to ride life and thrive within it.

If we were to choose one simple Laird take-away from his explorations of the roles and impact of death and fear in his life, it is his capacity for *keeping it real.*

But "keeping it real" is all too easy to say and not always so easy to do. So we have identified two key values of Laird's that might help guide our ability to do so. They are **commitment** and **humility**.

COMMITMENT

Absolute commitment to what's in front of him is one of Laird's core attributes. Whether it's a sixty-foot wave or a tree stump, a flood-threatened buffalo or a very irritable daughter, Laird does not go around or reverse from anything. He goes through it. As Gabby makes all too clear, "Laird's work rate is fucking insane."

This is Laird's point. Committing to the life in front of us both in the Now and in the future, without shying away or feinting, has nothing to do with boundless wells of strength, status, power, or intellect. Testing the edges of life and fully committing to what's in front of us does not rely on how many "likes" and "shares" we get.

If we fully commit to life as a creature and live within our limitations as an organism, traveling the road between birth and death with gusto and purpose, we can achieve extraordinary and remarkable things.

It is in that way that we become free. Only then do we realize that it is our embrace of the ordinary that presets us for extraordinary things. To willingly dive into the teeming multitude of banal actions and seemingly tiny undertakings that fill our days is what liberates us.

HUMILITY

To accept that we will die requires a supreme act of humility these days. And it's not hard to see why many of us struggle to find it.

We are being fed with convergent dreams of AI bringing us to a higher state of being and everlasting life. And while we're waiting, the lotions, potions, nips and tucks will stave off the rot of our coveted youth.

We increasingly adopt a swaggering arrogance in regard to ourselves and the world we live in. There is little humility in our belief that we can innovate our way out of anything from climate change, polluted air, and staggering poverty, to tsunamis of plastic in our oceans and microbeads in the fish we eat. We are gods bending physics to our will and transforming the material world in our image.

But to be capable of all of these things is to fundamentally miss the point.

Yes, we're amazing creatures in our ability to evolve and manage the environment around us and the manner in which we live, thrive, and survive in it. But Laird believes that we pollute our own great ideas, much like we do our planet, in selfish pursuits. And that has to do with hubris.

For Laird, the inability to find humility in the face of either metaphysical or scientific unknowns makes no sense.

By his own admittance, he has allowed hubris to shape his actions and his persona on occasion—but something within him has ultimately managed to grasp and hold on to the simple and powerful action of being humble.

'Ohana

Commitment and humility are core values of the Hawaiian *'ohana*. Each individual in the *'ohana* unit draws on the power of the Oneness of everything through their words and deeds, in every task they undertake—from lighting a fire, changing a tire, and clearing vegetation, to working the fields and fishing. They give thanks through *ho'oponopono*—mindful action. They invoke it to enable and empower their capabilities and competencies to mutual benefit. Every individual in that way commits to the others, and to the tasks the unit must perform in order to survive and thrive, both in itself and as one of multiple interconnected *'ohana* units, at any given time.

It is these individuals' unwavering commitment to each other and the task or challenge at hand that fuels their fierce application. In a way that some find surprising in a warrior people, arrogance and showiness are frowned upon as being un-Hawaiian.

There is a humility in the face of the great forces of nature and Oneness that guides their interactions with the people and natural world around them.

Humility is one of the sacred tenets of their worldview. It is always recognized and respected, even in the young, regardless of whether they themselves have achieved it or not. The issue in most Western societies is that we do not even recognize it anymore as a guiding principle. Humility, like decency and virtue, seems a little old-fashioned. In our newly accelerated state of being, such notions seem a little folksy and old-school—or there's a whiff of the hymnal about them.

Laird's commitment to the life he has, his family, and his community is immutable and nonnegotiable. Laird's humility toward his own failings and hubris is surprising given what he has achieved. That is how he keeps it real.

An Exercise in Keeping It Real

Once we commit to reality—to the immutable truth that we will one day die—and in turn therefore commit to the life we have, and not some fantasy or distant vision of what could be, we are freed to act in ways unfettered by the illusions and distractions that many of us wrestle with.

And once we realize that pride and hubris, and the arrogant delusion of superiority that accompany them, only lead to an inability to accept the fragility and fallibility of both ourselves and others, we can grasp the reality of our place among society and the creatures we share our homes, workplaces, and neighborhoods with.

Once all the esoteric conversation and theories are put aside, the question always is: *How is this relevant to me? How do I act on this in my everyday life?* So here's a small suggestion for how an act of commitment and humility can help you to keep stuff real.

Think of a person you have wronged. They may not even know that you have. An old high school friend. The lady at the corner shop. Your partner. Your child. That guy at work. Think of that person, and imagine how you might right the wrong— how you might make amends for it.

Imagine that, and then commit to it. Commit to it with fierce purpose. Put it on your "Things I must do before I die" list. Commit to it so that even if a hurricane is rumbling toward you or the sky is falling on your head, you will make amends. Whether it takes an hour, a month, a year, or a lifetime—commit to it.

And "wronged" is the key word here. Because to have wronged someone is to have acted in the absolute belief that you or what you were doing was right. Righteousness is a very destructive emotion. Righteousness does what it says on the box. It leads to a whole lot of people feeling *right*, because the device, book, or weapon in their hand tells them they are. And when so many people are busy being *right*, there is little room for wrong. And wrong is something we're all very capable of. The gift is in having the humility to both admit our wrongs and commit to correcting them.

HEART

"Our heart starts beating and
it doesn't stop until it's over."

—LAIRD HAMILTON

IN a world drowning in mindfulness and well-being mantras, it might be easy to overlook the heart.

In our concepts of ourselves as higher beings, the heart plays a very distant second fiddle to the human brain.

Increasingly the brain is everything, the super-processor of the super-protein computer that is us—and the heart is reduced to a biological algorithm that runs the machine that the brain directs.

But the heart's role in shaping our intuitive abilities, and in the balance of our emotional well-being, is far greater than we ever realized.

Advances in our understanding of the human heart are revealing it to be far closer in its nature to the holistic role afforded it by the ancients than the more one-dimensional version granted by recent biological science.

In this chapter, Laird explores the science and the psyche of the heart, not only in regard to our physiological evolution as individuals, but also in regard to its greater function at the core of the brilliant, sentient creatures we are.

In doing so, he reveals his own intimate feelings about how we tune, shape, and nurture our heart to play the preeminent role it deserves in a life fully lived—and what we lose by its narrow-minded dismissal to the sidelines.

LAIRD

In XPT terms, I connect heart to lung, so I give that a pretty good priority in training. Probably half to maybe three-quarters of my training goes to it. Everything at the end is always cardio-driven—heart-driven—when we're talking specifically about training.

Whenever we're going to the "wall" or we're going to "failure," the most commonly asked thing we get, in regard to performance and being in the water, is "How long can you hold your breath?"—and it's all relative to your heart rate. I can hold my breath for five minutes in the gym if I spend ten or fifteen minutes loading my lung up, lowering my heart rate, getting nice and calm; going into a meditation position.

But if you said, "Run across the yard as fast as you can and then hold your breath at the end," you'd be lucky to get thirty seconds. Maybe you'd be lucky to get twenty seconds. So a lot of what I have incorporated in all of my training is breath-focused. Whether I'm doing breath holding on cardio machines—inner breath training—or whether I'm doing all pool training; it's all based on a form of breath holding or hypoxic training [breath performance training based on reduced oxygen]. But always under supervision. It kind of protects you too, because you don't have the danger you do with free diving.

In free diving you try to lower your heart rate; you oxygenate and then you scrub your CO_2 and then you hyperventilate in order to see the CO_2 way down. But in doing that you lose the warning system that tells you to breathe—that forces you to breathe at the end of the breath cycle.

I prefer the other side of the scale—where I have high heart rate and the CO_2 levels aren't falsely scrubbed. Where you're not taking the level down through hyperventilation, which keeps the warning on. The red lights are flashing and you've got to breathe, and the demand to breathe is so great that you don't have to worry about shallow-water blackout—but again it's all connected to heart—your heart rate and your ability to control the relationship between heart and breathing.

I have a couple of philosophies about heart rate. One of them is that you need to keep it natural. There's a thing called "bonking" in sports [purposefully inducing hypoglycemia through training], where you are self-inducing failure. You are stressing the system so that you get to a point where you hit the wall, throw up, or have some form of extreme reaction. You would never see an animal in nature do that. I think that's a learned skill—a skill that we have actually developed through the lack of movement. That doesn't work for me. I don't do that.

What I've found, when I did monitor my heart rate, was that I naturally had this self-governing system, which seems to make more sense—that whenever my heart rate got too high it would just drop. It would naturally just descend, which would stop me from over-revving and ultimately failing.

In my world, I cannot afford a failure in the system. If I'm caught in a riptide and I'm swimming against it, if my heart rate went up to a maximal point and I threw up—I'd probably drown.

When I'm in a riptide and no one's around, I can't rely on anybody to save me because there is nobody to save me. In that moment I've got to save myself. If the system fails me, I go straight to death.

You need to develop a skill that's more in line with how our systems work naturally. Whether it's deep-sand running or nose breathing [in which oxygen is restricted and the heart rate elevates], 50 to 75 percent of my training is connected to the heart through cardio.

In XPT, in all of the pool work, you have a pretty elevated heart rate because you have elevated cardio, so anytime you get an exaggerated breath pattern, the heart's pounding to circulate the blood and oxygen to feed the muscles, to feed the system. Water makes a big difference—the pool environment, being in water, helps your system—your heart and your lungs—to self-regulate and find their rhythm.

The unique properties of water enable the heart to work more efficiently. The hydrostatic pressure of water . . . helps the heart circulate blood by aiding venous return (blood flow back to the heart). This . . . accounts for lower blood-pressure and heart rates during deep-water exercise. . . . Consequently, your heart rate is an estimated

10–15 beats lower per minute during suspended water exercise than for the same effort applied on land.

—P. E. DI PRAMPERO,

"THE ENERGY COST OF HUMAN LOCOMOTION

ON LAND AND IN WATER"

The inner relationship between breath and heart—that's a harmonious thing. The blood flows because the heart pumps it, and then the oxygen is absorbed through the lungs; so breath rate and breathing are directly connected to heart rate.

So bonking, or unrealistic heart-stressing, is not my thing, because I am trying to create a training scenario that's realistic to what I'm going to experience.

If I'm out there in big water, I'm not going to experience minimum heart rate from a meditative state. Just the physical act of being in giant surf is going to demand a very high heart rate, which at the end I need to prepare for, so an unnatural breath-holding technique isn't going to do shit for me when I have an elevated heart rate—unless I'm training for something that requires me to hold my breath within an elevated heart rate.

In big surf, heart is everything. You can feel it. When you're on the wave your heart is going like a trip-hammer. Let's face it, that shit is exciting. Super exciting. But that needs to be under control. You know why it's happening. There's a wave that you've waited for and trained for your whole life. And your heart's going to be in your mouth when it comes.

Everything's on. The sheer physical exertion of it is big. But it's more than that.

Your heart rate could be the excitement of just getting back to the peak to catch another wave—that whole antici-pation of riding another wave makes you just rev up.

Professional surfers, when actively riding a wave, main-tained . . . one of the highest, prolonged heart rate levels [for an endurance activity] (182±1.1 beats/min during 3 h of extreme surfing).

—WILLIAMS, BENGTSON, STELLER, CROLL, AND DAVIS,
"THE HEALTHY HEART: LESSONS FROM
NATURE'S ELITE ATHLETES"

I can use breathing techniques to help lower my heart rate and also replenish my oxygen. In the water you benefit from breathing techniques that you can use to help lower your heart rate quickly—calm yourself.

In my world that's a developed skill you need to know. You need to know what your system needs to do when you get wiped out. You get pounded by a wave and you get pushed down. Your body's self-defense mechanisms kick in: There's threat right there. There's risk. There's danger. You're an organism. You instantaneously get the possibil-ity of drowning. So you need to have prepared yourself—to make sure the right mechanisms kick in.

The wave hits. You go down. There are two things that need to happen. You have a super-high heart rate so you need to go instantly into calmness—relax everything, go to stillness. And you need to try to get your heart rate down as quickly as you can. Don't use your legs too much unless you really need to. Don't fight when the wave has you. Stay as calm as you can in order to get the longest amount of use from the oxygen that's in your system.

So in training we'll go from full speed, full rate, jacking the heart rate to the maximum, and then we go to stillness—to try to lower that thing as quickly as we can in order to get a lot of retention—because if you keep struggling and keep that heart rate revved, the oxygen can just be consumed instantaneously.

These are all forms of action that the organism knows. These are all things, responses, that are programmed into us—things I think we know and do innately. We just do it instinctually because the body's ability to tap into these kinds of self-protection are autonomic responses—beyond our conscious reflexes. The answer's in the word. They're "auto"—these things kick in automatically.

Is there one right way?

I think you develop different patterns and different skills and different techniques depending on what your exposures are—skills and responses required to survive the situation.

I think that at a certain point, the relationship with your heart—and your ability to create an awareness around how you can influence the autonomic system; an ability to apply decisions to it—becomes like a conscious awareness.

There's obviously ways in which, sometimes, we can induce the autonomic system response—through manual techniques. But they aren't pure. In a forced or cultivated situation, you don't have all the elements that you need for the autonomic response to be triggered in its purest sense.

If I'm not in big surf getting pounded, my autonomic system is probably going to have a different kind of response to what happens, even when I stress my heart in a pool environment.

You can have autonomic responses that you can cultivate in controlled environments, but I have a feeling that to trigger the real depth of autonomic response you need the whole scenario. That's what gives the organism the information it needs to throw the switch. It gives context. I have a feeling that I'm able to do things in the surf and in the waves that I just don't or can't do anywhere else, even if I try to.

That could just be my ability to be more comfortable in that situation than other people. Everybody can go into the pool. We can all do the same training, where basically everything's the same, but then you go into the surf— into a situation I intuitively and instinctively know as an organism—and it has a different effect on my autonomic system, and I respond differently.

Obviously we know we can develop parts of those skills and become more refined at it—but it's part of a highly developed complex organic system. One that's been honed over millions of years. We've been "raised" in an environment where threat was a natural condition for us. A natural existence.

If you're going to throw the switches, part of what you need, ultimately, is the true threat. As an evolved organism, you have a different gear when you experience true threat— way more than you do when you have the self-imposed threat of a cultivated environment.

Your autonomic system is geared to go to the max when you have an exterior threat that's real. All of our sensory systems, all the early-warning systems we have, are tuned, programmed to recognize true threat and respond.

Your system is not going to opt you out when the threat's an exterior one—you don't have the option, because there is no option.

I definitely know there are practices that will improve your technique—to hone or influence the autonomic response. The work that we do with XPT is designed to do that.

We use the mind as an override switch. A lot of it is in the mind—so the mind stuff we do is about its role in stressing the system—the mental difficulty of sitting in the ice and staying there—the mental job of holding your breath underwater with weights. A lot of these things are mental things—they're physical acts but they're physical acts to induce mental stimuli.

And they're a beautiful thing. Your shock in the ice—your discomfort in the heat—your fear in the water—your breath panic. That's a beautiful thing because that's going to induce transformation—that panic and that shock are going to invite transformation. You're going to transform from that. You're going to wake up the systems, wake up the organism.

However varied in capability everyone seems when they arrive at the pool, once everybody's "awake," we're all really not that far from each other.

Some people have had more exposure to it; they've already been exposed to the environments which might have switched them "on" a little—or a lot.

They could arrive with breath awareness. They might have a thing with the heat—they might have a thing with the ice—if you're comfortable in the water then you don't have the shock of it. If you spend any time in the ice, you don't have the shock of that.

So we seek out the shock—the stress points—to help the organism wake up.

If you haven't spent any time in that ice, when you get in, you've got an immediate autonomic response: to get out. BANG!—the shock hits and you just start hyperventilating. You want to get out of that thing because the system knows it's dangerous. Your highly evolved organism recognizes the threat—freezing water equals heart failure— system failure. *This is a bad environment.* This is no different to any other threat stimulus. I see a spider. I see a snake. My evolved, threat-aware, danger-averse responses tell me: *These are dangerous things: get away from them.*

These are threats that have been pretty effective in hurting the organism over our evolutionary lifetime as a species. So we automatically respond to them.

That's the mental part of heart, cardio, and endurance training. Once you stop and override that immediate flight response, the organism goes up a gear. The organism thinks, *OK, well I'm not getting out of the ice—even though I'm hyperventilating and that would normally have me out of here—now I'm not—so now you've got me—so I will get my shit together— I've got to survive being in here—so I've got to regulate the hormones. I'm going to lower the rates on everything. I'm going to bring the blood into the organs. I'm going to just scramble and do all the things that I need to do now to endure the environment.*

When we don't react to the first self-defensive response of *get out of the freezing water,* we go to the second one, which is to organize ourselves in order to endure being in that environment. This is where all the transformation happens.

But if I want to point to a focus, as an organism, it all comes back to the heart. In everything we do, we're catering to the heart. When I say, "Hey, nose breathing will get you through this," I'm saying that because it will bring your heart rate down. We breathe to calm our heart.

Everything is ultimately connected to the heart, because the heart is primary. Everything is in service to the heart. Even our gut and its central role as the sensory echo chamber for our subconscious organism—in primary terms, for me it's the heart. And there's a very good reason for that. Rooted in our evolution—how we've developed as a species.

There was a time when you could get through all kinds of other shit. You could be knocked in the head pretty good and have brain damage but survive. But if you had catastrophic heart stuff you didn't live. You can have half a lung and you could kind of make it, but you can't have a half a heart.

Our heart is a pretty primary piece of the organism. Our survival depends on it. Not just mechanically. It's a pretty crazy piece of engineering. It's an amazing thing. The heart is "connected." And it connects us. To ourselves, to those around us.

Our heart is connected to our intuition, and it's connected to our feelings. What's on every Valentine's Day card? Love and the heart. That's not just Hallmark making shit up. They print that stuff because we believe that stuff. And we believe that stuff because it's true. The reason that a heart symbolizes what it is to be human is because it brings together both sides of us—it's what connects the science and the spirit.

Far more than a mechanical pump, the heart functions as a sensory organ and as a complex information encoding and processing center. Groundbreaking research in the relatively new field of neurocardiology [by pioneering researcher Dr. J. Andrew Armour] has demonstrated that the heart has an extensive intrinsic nervous system that is sufficiently sophisticated to qualify as a "little brain" in its own right. . . . Containing over 40,000 neurons, its complex circuitry enables it to sense, regulate, and remember. Moreover, the heart brain can process information and make decisions about cardiac control independently of the central nervous system (Armour, 2003; Armour & Kember, 2004).

—MCCARTY, ATKINSON, TOMASINO & BRADLEY,
THE COHERENT HEART: HEART-BRAIN INTERACTIONS,
PSYCHOPHYSIOLOGICAL COHERENCE, AND
THE EMERGENCE OF SYSTEM-WIDE ORDER

Sure, we can do amazing things these days. We can transplant mechanical hearts, sew and splice bits of them into us. Perhaps that's why when someone's in a coma we become so emotionally ripped up. It's confusing.

I've always traditionally connected the heart and breath to life. If your heart's not beating, you know that you're dead. So then you go into the other part of it—consciousness. The system's working and the heart can actually keep the body alive without the brain. But the spirit, the soul's not there.

I had that with my mom.

So I get how the brain acts in us. And I get why, in our computational age, the brain is everything. The brain computes real easy if you're viewing the world through algorithms. But consciousness is not the brain. Intuition is not the brain. Those things are a whole different level.

Intuition is a way in which our unconscious self applies itself in our conscious world. It's like an interpreter for the organism. It turns all of this unseen information and activity into something we can comprehend and do something with. There's more to us than just a brain wired into a protein machine.

Perhaps, when you hear about this stuff, these events where someone has been in a brain-dead coma—no signals, no responses, no nothing—and then they come out of it— you wonder.

Who knows? Was the "little brain" they talk about working all that time? Collecting data; feeling; functioning? Holding it together in there while the brain scraped itself out. Or mended itself?

So I think we're past the old mechanics of heart as a pump, a piece of plumbing. We're way past that. So now we're like back to the future. The future of heart medicine is going to be way wider, way broader.

All that stuff about soul and spirit and feeling, and the science of us as an organism, is going to just join up. Joining the dots.

You know what it feels like when you have a broken heart, right? You know what that sensation is—you feel the pain very clearly. The loss. All those feelings and memories and sensations and intimacies. All that stuff. And where does it hurt? Right here. Heart is everything. Like a big intersection.

We feel things in our heart not just for sentimental reasons. We physically "feel" things in our heart because it's responding to everything around us. Yes, it's running the ship, keeping us alive. But we're alive because of it in a far bigger way. We feel because of it. It's like a beacon and a compass stuck together. There is an electromagnetic field around the human heart. A field that recognizes, responds to, and interacts with other fields. Other hearts. That's not fluffy stuff. That's rooted in the science of us.

> The heart generates the largest electromagnetic field in the body . . . about 60 times greater in amplitude than the brain waves recorded in an electroencephalogram (EEG) . . . and can be measured several feet away from the body. . . . [And] it is possible for the magnetic signals radiated by the heart of one individual to influence the brain rhythms of another.
>
> —ROLLIN MCCRATY, "THE ENERGETIC HEART:
> BIOELECTROMAGNETIC COMMUNICATION
> WITHIN AND BETWEEN PEOPLE"

The role of heart as the meeting point between our physical and metaphysical selves: that's ancient. That belief lies at the heart of almost every civilization for a reason. We know it intuitively. And that's what I mean when I say it either all comes back to math, or it is something that we're perhaps never going to know. And that's OK. But this stuff is real.

Stuff happens between people, and between people and environments. And energy lies at the heart of that. And right there, at the center of that physical energy, is the heart.

You know if all that stuff is going on at the earth's core. Electromagnetic fields and pulses and waves of massive

LAIRD

scale. And if this is an energy that other creatures can feel and sometimes see, up here on the surface and alive in the ocean, well, the ocean is a pretty big superconductor. That water is alive with it.

Why do I know that? Because my instinct tells me it's true. When I get in the ocean, something happens. And my heart's at the center of that. Get inside a wave and that's intimacy beyond explanation. And that's about more than just the experience and the emotion of being inside a living tunnel of water—that's an exchange of energy right there.

The ancients understood this stuff. And then we got knowledge—and the more we got knowledge, the more we just moved away from the ancient view of heart at the center of everything—we moved to the brain as master. "Hey, look at us. We're humans. Look at the size and capacity of our brains." We let ego disconnect us. We lost heart in more ways than one.

The Hawaiian word for the heart, "pu'uwai,"—literally "lump of water,"—referring to the ancient Polynesian concept of the heart as the primary matter (lump) representation of the sources of basic life-sustaining energy (water).

—PAUL PEARSALL, THE HEART'S CODE

There's a reason for why we say "that guy's got heart" when we're referring to someone's ability to go the distance.

There's a reason why when referring to the absolute fundamentals—the absolute focus—of something, we say "to get to the heart of the matter." Because as an organism, that's what we understand through experience. The heart is central and primary. It's proven itself over time to be true.

At the end of the long trek or whatever, you're running on empty, you're close to the end—and your brain just wants to stop but your heart is where your focus goes; the one final reserve that you go to—you grab from the heart. It is what separates you from other people and their ability to drive the car, right?

Your relationship with the heart is central. The heart of a man is the center—that's your core.

Everything is connected to it. In service to it. There's a reason for that. Beyond the mechanics. That oxygenation—and the fact is that you can control heart rate—slow your breath down and the heart rate will slow down—all of that is in service to the core of the organism. The primary ruler.

The lungs and the heart have a very unique relationship—it's unlike any other two organs. Yes, the other organs have a relationship with the heart because they are being fed by the heart—maintained by it—but the relationship between the lungs and the heart is a very special relationship.

When I think of that relationship I think of the heart as ruler and the lungs as healer. The heart is always central, more than any other organ, for both our physical and emotional well-being. And I try to respect that, not only in how I train but in how my relationships play out.

My personal life, my relationship with Gabby, with the kids, with my friends, with the guys around the pool. That's as important to my heart health as my XPT pool training.

[In Hawaiian culture and belief systems the heart resides in the lower soul—the *unihipili*.] The basic self, in fact, controls the body: the musculature, the internal organs, the five senses, and the autonomic nervous system. It is the seat of the emotions, memory, instinct, and survival. . . . It also provides information about the body itself through energy level, heart rate, temperature, pleasure, and pain. It utilizes vital life force or mana to perform all of these functions.

—CHARLOTTE BERNEY,

FUNDAMENTALS OF HAWAIIAN MYSTICISM

That stuff has to have the right balance. If it's just fitness or exercise you're missing something pretty fundamental, right there.

That's why we say XPT is a lifestyle—not just fitness. Yes, its fitness, there's working out. But there's community in it. There's all these things that go way beyond fitness and exercise. Ultimately it's lifestyle—which means it's about how to live your life in a style by which it is connected to everything—to your autonomic system—to your mind—to your heart—it's connected to all these things.

That thing of family, *'ohana*. I suppose we create that in our lives, including everyone and everything in that. A sense of family—and how that matters. How you look out for each other, how you work with each other, and the life you make.

"I think that's one thing that's hard for him, I think that having three daughters that you just can't control and where there's been some events that you know are heartbreaking, and I see Laird suffer because he can't fix it.

"His first reaction is to just sort of go at it, like 'OK, I'm gonna fix it,' and he can't. It's pretty astounding but I think he gets heartbroken. I do think he gets heartbroken. I think he feels things deeper than most."

—GABBY REECE

And you don't do that in isolation. We are social creatures. We have evolved with each other. Together. That's how we have evolved as a species. I can't be whole if I haven't tended to every spoke in the wheel—the people I love, my friends, my community, my people. If my heart, my emotions, aren't being given as much effort as my body, I'm incomplete. The spokes of the wheel are incomplete. And if the spokes of the wheel are incomplete, the wheel just collapses. It's that "little brain" thing. Everything is connected. And the heart is at the heart of it.

"To be a warrior, one must truly be compassionate. Laird has that in spades. If someone needs help, it never even occurs to him to think about it—that's what you do. If someone is hurt or suffers or has something, Laird feels it—and he can be a dick too!

"He can be insensitive—and he can sometimes sense that you have a weakness—and he'll just fucking jab it—if it's something that he doesn't understand or it doesn't vibrate with him. Sometimes he says things that are so uncomfortable—so unwrapped. He doesn't put a bow on it."

—GABBY REECE

So many guys are like, "Hey, I'm the alpha guy, right? I'm the big dog." And you say something to them that involves emotion, you express some real emotion, something deep, and the look on their face is like, *Huh?* Like, *Are we really talking about this stuff?* Feelings are like Kryptonite to guys like that. For them that's weakness right there. But for me that's not weakness. For me, denying one's feelings is one bad strategy for survival. That's a bad strategy for winning.

One of my favorite books, *Natural Born Heroes* by Christopher McDougall, cites one thing as the greatest mark of a leader: compassion. Not courage. Not strength. Not endurance. But compassion. That's heart right there. At the center of it.

You can be the biggest, baddest dog, but if you haven't got compassion you haven't got shit. And compassion takes awareness. Compassion takes heart.

If you don't *feel* and *do* with all your heart, I think you're going to fail—I think you're going to lose. "All your heart" means just that—all of it. The intuitive, the emotional, the physical, the psychological. That means having compassion, always. You don't have to take a bath in it. But you've got to have it. And that's courage. To show compassion, to bring it into even the gnarliest of situations, you have to be brave. You have to go first with your heart. Put it out there. Raw. True.

"I don't know if you noticed—but Laird has incredibly feminine eyes. They're highly feminine. They're highly sensitive. I mean they can be like a wild animal but they're still very feminine, and for me it always speaks to how developed that side of the spirit is—the emotional side. And he's far more sensitive than I am. He's the most grateful of everybody."

—GABBY REECE

So in the end, sure, work out and do live how you want to and it's going to help you. For me that had an effect—the extreme physicality—but in the end that's so limiting. And it's not real.

You need depth. Like emotional depth. I see people come through our Xtreme Performance Training Program and they are affected profoundly. You see the transformation. You see their face and they're like, "I got it. I got woke up." Now, what you do with the new you once you've woken up the organism is up to you, that's your deal, but we've helped you discover that part of you that has been sleeping—or perhaps you've been using it, but you haven't been in touch with it as deep as you could be. As I said, some people arrive with some sense of what's in the tank—and some don't.

"It struck me how tender Laird is. There is a gentleness I've seen.

"When I think about the room and how much love is there—it's like when Laird says, 'Look at that pool. That pool is full of mana [the vital life force in Hawaiian mysticism]—you just feel so good here—we fill that pool with mana.' There's a physical reality that transforms this very water, or is it more the spirit in the people in the pool?"

—RANDALL WALLACE,
SCREENWRITER AND XPT PARTICIPANT

The people we train are going to go deeper and continue to learn—continue to evolve, continue to explore themselves. That's XPT—it's a total exploration of the self. Sure we do breath work, we do cardio, we do hydrostatic workouts, we do hot boxing and ice—but we also do community stuff, just being together, and we go to nature—and we have speakers that give us information and the inspiration to go find other aspects of our life, of ourselves.

We explore nutrition and hydration and all those other tools that you need to assist the heart—to continue to service the heart in all its dimensions. Not just some pump workout.

We service the heart with our eating, we service the heart with our thoughts, we service the heart with our breath, we service the heart with our heat, with our ice, with our swimming, with our running. With everything.

Because the heart rules, right?

BAREFOOT BUSINESS

Heart & the power of the Why

If you were looking for a bull's-eye in regard to the tipping point between success and failure in business, the Why is a pretty good place to start.

Mission-led businesses cite clarity of purpose—beyond the balance sheet and the material and physical nature of the operation of the business—as the single defining factor in how they continue to thrive.

Knowing what gets you up in the morning, and why you do what you do, can create a paradigm shift in focus, performance, culture, and outcomes for both the individual entrepreneur and the executive council of a large corporation.

Purpose creates clarity around everything from innovation to HR to operational efficiencies to customer insight. It is a North Star for everyone to follow.

Here, Laird and Gabby talk about how knowing yourself, and being clear about why you do what you do, is the greatest source of resilience in any business; and they discuss the benefits and rewards such clarity can bring.

LAIRD

Everything that I'm involved in has a pretty authentic connection to me.

All the businesses that I'm involved in are a reflection of needs of mine. They're all authentic to me. If I don't use it, wear it, ride it, eat it, or believe it, then I'm not in it.

All the equipment is based around equipment that I use, or based around equipment that I've been developing for other people to use.

XPT is my lifestyle, and everything attached to it is a reflection of that lifestyle; so every single thing is authentic. I am not involved in anything on a strictly financial investment basis. If the objective is to make money, then you might as well be making money from things that you believe in. Everything that I'm involved in has something to do with health and wellness and being active.

The GolfBoard we designed with BMW is really just a way to make golfing more exciting, more interesting, something I would want to do more of. Take a board, stick an engine on it, and I'm surfing the golf course.

The GolfBoard business is more conceptual for me. I act as a figurehead for that but I have minimal participation. I have a hard-goods equipment project around stand-up paddle boards and my new eFoil, I have the Superfood project, the apparel project. And then we have XPT, which is the experiential health and wellness, lifestyle, and fitness project.

Everything is an authentic reflection of my philosophy—my lifestyle. Somewhere in each one is the DNA of my beliefs—otherwise I just don't do it. And that includes companies that I am associated with, like Land Rover or Yamaha. Even the sponsors we collaborate with have an authentic connection to me. That isn't always at a practical or application level. Sometimes it might just be at a corporate philosophy level.

There's a lack of sincerity in the world because a lot of people are just out to make stuff. "Hey, I'm making some weird device to make money," and then it's this whole disconnect to doing things out of a misplaced interest in money.

I think all the greatest ideas and all the successful businesses came from people's genuine passion for something. Take companies like Apple or Google—they started with real authenticity. Where it goes from there, and why they might lose their way, is a different thing. But in their beginning—there is authentic passion. Genuine feeling.

If there is an authentic purpose, it makes it a lot easier to be passionate about it. And you'll put time into it. And you'll give it the effort that it needs.

I still believe that you can do good and be successful. Make money, do good. How do you actually make good things happen for people through your products? It tends to come every time for people who are very authentic and true to what they've done.

And why would you waste your life doing anything else? There's not enough time in the day to waste it on things that aren't good for you and you don't believe in.

You don't have enough time in a lifetime to just think that you got time to go and put energy into something that doesn't have some sort of benefit or the ability to make an improvement in the world—or that is just making you a better person.

The fact is, you'll feel good about things—if you're projecting good out, then it will make you feel good.

For example, now that there is awareness for my brand, I can participate in trying to produce boards.

But we need somebody that can distribute them. In that way it becomes a similar deal to apparel, where we need a strategic partner that can handle all the infrastructure and distribution, because just building that aspect of the business alone takes particular experience and skills. I just don't have the years or the expertise to do it. That's the thing where you need focus and clarity. You need to focus on your strengths, and bring in experts early on in the areas you just don't know about or have weakness in.

You have to decide. Certain businesses you might build from scratch, like the Creamer for Superfood—because you can build distribution online.

But it's going to be hard to distribute boards online. You have to accept that each business has unique complications because of the nature of them.

And if you want to run multiple businesses, you're going to need that authenticity to see you through. It acts like a spine through everything. A strength. And you're going to need it. Because running multiple businesses requires a lot.

Each one could have a different strategic partner in that business.

If you're making GolfBoards for golf courses, it doesn't just stop at designing and fabricating the boards. You need salesmen to sell boards at golf courses and try to get golf courses to buy. That's very different from having your Creamer range online, or having Barneys carry your apparel, or having REI carry your hard goods. Or bringing people through an experiential health and wellness program.

The strategic partner for each one of those could be different.

Sometimes people think that if you just get some capital, that's enough. Capital can be enough if you have the time and you have the know-how, but with some of these projects you just don't have this ability to just wait indefinitely—at some point the product has to be pushed into the market.

And it also depends on the maturity of the business.

GolfBoards is a surviving business. It's trying to infiltrate the golf-course market. We're actually trying to develop some different boards for outside of the golf course—into resorts—and adventure boards. But it's at a stage right now where we're building them in the UK and it's extremely expensive. It puts the cost of goods at a real high point, which limits the entry level, so we're looking for new manufacturing in that business.

Right now I have the most heart and passion for my superfood business, because that has been most successful. I'm also passionate about XPT, because it's promoting a healthy lifestyle and it really has a huge impact on people. But that one doesn't have the reach that the superfood business does. The superfood business has so much reach on it—so many possibilities—we can really push that.

Ultimately, if I have some success and the business benefits me, that benefits the girls. It gives me an ability to be there for them and help them in a way financially that I wouldn't if it wasn't successful—but I'm not saying it's *just* for them because that wouldn't be honest. It is for us— Gabby and I—besides being a tool to help other people.

For me, business is also about belief. I'm not interested in pursuing things just for the money. I'm interested in pursuing things that are powered by belief—that's part of the experience of life.

If you conceptually believe this is something special and you have this belief, then the success of it solidifies your belief; it confirms it.

A little bit like stand-up paddling. Even when no one was interested, I believed in it. Now everybody's doing it, all over the world. That's a kind of confirmation that it's something special.

We need to allow our intuition to go to work. In business as in life. We need to allow the natural course of things.

How much time and attention we invest in something is testament to its value. The things that demand more time, that will benefit from it, will make themselves known to you. If you're putting a bunch of time into something that's not having success, then you have to ask yourself if that's the best use of your time. If it's not paying dividends, then you might have to question the volume of effort put in.

But more than time and effort, I understand the necessity of setting clear priorities. That's kind of obvious—but I have to. In my world, on the water, priorities make or break you. So you learn real fast that they're not a "nice to have." If you lose sight of your priorities in the ocean, you can get in trouble real quick. In that way, riding life and riding a wave are no different.

So even in regards to my businesses, I put health at the top. Because without my health, everything else is compromised. Without an optimum level of health, I can't do anything, because everything is connected. My businesses are an extension of what I do on and in the water. So the same priorities apply.

You hear some people say, "Unless I can put 110 percent into something, I don't want to do it at all." That's like the textbook hard-ass approach. "Extreme business." Every hour, every second, devoted to the business. But I would question what that 110 percent really looks like. How productive is that workaholic?

If you're not really maximizing your health, your physicality and your mental state, the number of man-hours you put into a project is irrelevant. I'll take four hours of someone's best work over eight hours of their kind of average.

That's always the question: How much time do you really need to spend on a project if that time is smart and precisely used? If you really care about your products and quality and customer service, why pay bottom dollar for more low-quality time from underperforming people?

Pay top dollar for less time. Get smart. But it's about more than just smarts.

It's about respecting people's value. If you want people to go the extra mile, respect is critical.

Make sure you surround yourself with high-quality people that get you, because you have to delegate no matter what. No matter who you are, you're going to have to do a certain amount of delegation—so what does that look like? And what's the work rate of the people you're delegating to?

Do you have five hundred people that are operating at 75 percent, or do you have a hundred people that are operating at 150 percent? It's like, do you know what you know? And do you do all that you can do? And that means getting your hands dirty.

Too many people forget what it is to dig the dirt. Or they never had to.

I like to continue to put my hands in the dirt, just to be reminded about the effort it takes to do this task or that, and so I can respect and appreciate people that are doing that.

And that appreciation has to come from a position of understanding instead of just "Oh yeah, I can relate to what that takes." Well, no, you can't really relate to what that takes until you actually do it—so are you willing to go down there and scrub the toilet and say, "Wow, scrubbing the toilet, that takes effort"? Do that yourself and you can sympathize with the people that do that.

And when it's personal, when it's authentic and it's yours, you don't have the luxury of mediocrity that big business has.

Everything has to be super-tuned. Everybody has to be super-tuned. And a believer.

I mean, you give people a chance but you instinctively know—you intuitively know what their potential is. It doesn't take much to understand people. What do they say? "Give people that are busy things to do, because they are doing things—and people that aren't busy? Don't give them anything to do, because they're not doing anything."

Why are people available? Because they don't have anything else going on—that's why they're available. When you're forced into positions where you might have to delegate, the biggest part of making that a success is that, regardless of whether you would do it differently or not, you have to be willing to let them do it the way they do it.

And that's a little bit of what you give up by not doing it yourself—that you're going to go, "Hey, they're not going to do it like I do it. I have to be willing to accept the fact that they're going to do it the way they want to do it."

If you don't like that truth, you're going to keep getting somebody else to do it differently until a point comes where they do it in a way you like. And you have to wonder at that point whether that was a smart use of your and everyone else's time.

I think that there's a lot of luck involved in who you partner with and how they fit in—because one person in one position at one business might be the wrong one, and that same person at another business could be the perfect one for it. So to know that intuitively—that's a real art. And probably people with huge success can sense that intuitively.

When that intuition fails you, that's the most difficult part. Telling people, "Hey, sorry." That's the hardest thing to do.

LAIRD / BAREFOOT BUSINESS

But, thinking on it, it's not the most *destructive* thing to do. The most destructive thing to do is just let them continue on—and not say something.

I think sometimes people have a tendency to not want to say anything, and don't want to hurt the feelings of someone, but that is going to compromise the success of whatever you're doing.

It's exactly like a relationship. You have to be able to tell people straight, because otherwise you're going to waste your time and their time.

And this is all just part of the territory. If you're going to do this stuff, you have to have the heart for it. All of it. The good and the bad.

GABBY

Laird's sense of purpose is there all the time when it comes to riding waves, and our family and our relationship—but that's obviously different in business. What he is 100-percent sure about and feels in charge of—even if he has to wait for it—is riding waves.

I think with the businesses, his purpose is less intimate, you know, but it is as productive. And it's constant. It will always get to a point where he'll generate an idea either on purpose or by accident.

Like the Creamer—that was like a real hobby as far as appreciating coffee, as well as also being connected into the understanding that coffee can be used in performance and health.

When this originally started, it was just something he

got jacked up on in the morning. Then I think as he got educated and as he went deeper, it became way more important to him. We started having beans flown in from places all the time.

We can be in the most remote place in mud and rain, and you know, beautiful beans are showing up. So it's a really genuine interest and passion. Then, as it geared towards performance and what he was putting in his body, for Laird it became an even more important story—and suddenly there's a business.

There's no flaky stuff with Laird. When he does have to show up for business stuff, he always over-delivers—in any of these things, whether it's a book signing or XPT. Laird can't help himself. He's always going to give everything he has, but don't ask him to do that all the time unless it's riding waves or being with his family. That's the thing he knows that feeds him. He's smart enough to think, *OK, let's say I forgo some of my time riding waves, or being in the ocean itself, for developing things, to build a monster business, to make lots of money; will I be happier?*

He knows the answer. His heart wouldn't be in it. So he's not even seduced by that idea, because I don't think it feels like that's who he is to himself.

He is generous in everything. Think about stand-up paddling—Laird is the person who, whether it's existed before or not, brought it into the modern era—with modern equipment.

He was the one—and he didn't really monetize that, and I think because it's so secondary for him, he just wanted to do stand-up paddleboarding and he wanted the best stuff to do it.

It has been the business that he's made the least amount of money in, so it's an interesting example of how his desire, his purpose, isn't driven by money stuff.

A lot of times when he does things it's because he wants it and it doesn't exist, or something does exist but it isn't good enough—that's really what it comes down to. Innovation with Laird is driven by need and function. Not just some kind of vanity.

Like when Will, our partner in Laird Apparel, put stainless steel threading in the shorts. Because it's innovative and cool? Sure. But to be fair, it's mainly because Laird rips all his shorts and they needed to be stronger.

It's really quite simple that way. The reason for building the first stand-up paddleboards? He needed the boards and nobody had the boards. Quickblade made the paddles because they had to be longer but lighter—because the regular person couldn't carry a long wooden paddle.

So I have to say that with the businesses—some are a passion expanded, some are the equipment Laird is seeking, and other times I would almost say it's Laird doing and connecting an idea or it coming to him.

So that's the need or passion driving them. A strong desire. But I will say that the other side of that, and this is another part of Laird, is that he gets an enormous amount of enjoyment from seeing people love what he's created or done.

The other day I was leaving the beach in a real surfers' location—and these are the higher-performing surfers, the better surfers in the world—and as I was leaving I passed by all the trucks and one truck had a Laird board in it, and I passed by and the next truck had a Laird board in it, and then another, and another.

I think for Laird the notion of people coming up and saying how much they enjoy the boards, or the Creamer, I think he gets a real sense of enjoyment out of figuring something out or having helped figure something out—and then other people going "I really like it," or "It really helps me," or "It makes me feel good."

I think he takes real pleasure in that because, in a way, that's the only way he's going to connect with most people.

Understand: Laird's a reluctant participant at times. It's connected to his defiance—his "I don't want to be told what to do."

It's just an innate thing in him, but this side of things brings out something in him. There's a creative element to doing a business that he really does enjoy—and having those kinds of reactions really gives him a charge.

But business for business's sake? With no passion or heart? He's not interested.

He has a great deal of humility. He doesn't live in a bubble. He's in the mud; he's riding his tractor; he's getting smashed by waves. You know, Laird could have money trees in his yard, and that just wouldn't make him be any different—because that's who he is.

Recently I did ask Laird, "If Nestlé or someone says, 'We want to buy your stuff—we'll buy you out! We'll give you a hundred million dollars, you personally, and you'll get paid a licensing fee to use your name for the Creamer,' would you sell the whole business? Or would you sell less of your business, and take a little less, to maintain ownership? To make sure you'll still be involved in the process?"

And he's like, "Yes. Sell less. Stay involved." I already knew the answer but I was just curious—because I think that's an important thing for people—where they are at on that.

Especially now, in this tech world, and all this crazy unicorn stuff, where all these companies are being bought up for crazy money—"Oh, they bought them for a billion, they bought them for $500 million."

It's very cliché, but I think people equate money and success with happiness. But what then? So, I sell the business I've built and then I start to realize, hmm, what next? If you've built a business, then you probably like solving problems, creating things, collaborating, growing things, and all of the stuff that comes with it. Trying, failing; trying, succeeding.

I think that this, in a way, brings a far richer human experience.

The money's great—it's security, it's opportunity, it's mobility, it's freedom. It's all these things, but I think certainly Laird is connected enough to know, like—that's not going to do it.

So you see Laird and go, "Hi, I'm the CEO of the company and I make $25 million a year," and Laird's like, "Hmmmm." What he admires is "I built something. I made something."

If you said, "I built this app and I sold the company for two billion dollars," I don't think he would be interested. Now, if you said the app gets food that's left unused and gets it sent to people that are hungry, then he might go, "OK—now I'm listening." But if it's an app to give you the best restaurants in a four-mile radius, I don't think he cares.

It's not like we haven't been around people that have it all—whether it's the fame, the power, whatever. And you look around and you go, "OK—that's not the full answer. Those things are not a route to contentment."

Laird is a smart person and I don't think he ever wants to just be identified as just a surfer, in that way. There's other thoughts, there's other interests that fire his heart. That's where he is.

Work Your Empathy

Our heart is a powerful thing. But it pumps more than just oxygenated blood. The heart has sat at the center of almost every belief system since humans started forming them. It was seen as our primary and most powerful nexus. But our current assertion of the mind's preeminence—both as the killer app of human evolution and the portal to potential happiness—has led us away from the primacy of the heart. We've become somewhat blind to the sublime intricacies of its workings and effect. It's a pump we exercise in a spinning class or a cardio workout. But to think of it that way is to miss more than half of the puzzle, as far as Laird is concerned.

Laird has a "big" heart, by just about every measure you can imagine.

He is very clear on how his heart acts as an emotional centrifuge in the turbulence of life. And on how staying true to it is one of the hardest things we can do.

In revealing that the heart is central to our autonomic system, science tells us that it is a fundamental element in our intuitive self—a part of our sentient, conscious being.

Intuition is one of the most powerful facets of our creature selves. Intuition charges our existence. It is one of the lights within us that make us brilliant in the truest sense of the word.

Our sense of spirit and resilience are powered directly by it. When we say someone "has heart," we don't just mean they have a valved pump that distributes oxygenated blood around the body. We mean they have the spirit to persevere and prevail. They have the ability to absorb turbulence and volatility—take the knocks—without losing their desired state. In everyday terms, that translates into: *How do I get through a world of pain or endure extreme conditions emotionally, physically, and spiritually without losing myself in the process? How do I maintain my desired sense of purpose and uphold my beliefs and values in the middle of a storm? How do I take the knocks and get back up again with my soul intact?*

If the heart is not optimal, then the intuitive system is not optimal. If the intuitive system is not optimal, we are underperforming at the conscious level. We do not have the spiritual strength and resilience to persevere, even if we have the physical reserves of Atlas. We lose the ability our intuitive self brings us to remain—even under extreme duress—a caring, considerate human being who is aware of others and our effect and impact upon them.

So one thing we can take from this chapter is that, in stressing his heart through cardio performance, Laird isn't just seeking optimal physical performance; he is also seeking his optimal intuitive and empathetic self. He is *exercising his emotional intelligence.*

And the two values that seem to sit at the center of emotional intelligence are **performance** and **compassion**.

PERFORMANCE

Cardio is the heart of Laird's exercise regime. As he states: "Everything is in service to the heart." What we eat, how we eat, how we sleep, when we sleep, who we love, how we love, how socialized we are, how happy in our work we are, how introspective we are, and how open we are—but the greatest invigoration of the heart, in its fullest sense, comes down to not only how much and how often we move—but to what we move *through*.

According to Laird, exercise is always enriched and amplified by the physical context in which that exercise happens—by the space through which you choose to move. It's hard to feel elated beyond the endorphin rush in an indoor gym or workout space—but in an outdoor pool, through a park, up a hill, through snow, along a hillside path, among trees? The simple cardio exercise of moving through spaces where you "feel" the environment around you becomes heightened, because the expansiveness of the feeling draws the intuitive self into the process. Moving through nature, whether on land or on sea, triggers deeper mechanisms in us that help to both stress and regulate the heart's performance. For Laird, the heart's physical activity needs to have context. It needs to have purpose. And it needs to be meaningfully connected to the other aspects of our system—the autonomic, the intuitive.

A heart performing at maximum capacity and potential keeps Laird at the peak of the experience, fueling the parts of his system that keep him conscious to an exceptional degree.

COMPASSION

Laird repeatedly refers to the virtue of compassion. It is the most significant takeaway from one of his favorite books, *Natural Born Heroes*. Leadership and the heroic ideal are powered not by strength, cunning, stealth, or old-school IQ, but by compassion. The others are important traits in the heroic ideal but compassion supercedes them all. To be able to remain compassionate—considerate, empathetic, and sympathetic—even in the face of extreme depredation, tyranny, aggression, futility, hunger, thirst, fear, or ultimately death—requires a resilience that few of us would claim to have.

When Laird says someone has heart, he means they have all of the qualities required to exercise their compassion in any and every eventuality. To Laird, this is greatness. And to be all of those things, and relentlessly so, requires us to be "on." To be all of those things, our intuition needs to be primed and tuned to perform at its greatest capacity. In that way, our capacity for compassion is inextricably linked to the physical condition of our heart.

Without performance at its most basic level and compassion at its rarest level, we struggle to walk the turbulent path between chaos and order.

'Ohana

Performance is a given in Hawaiian culture, which values both the individual and collective undertakings of its people highly. It is a culture of "doing." Of application and fierce purpose. *'Ohana*, the extended family, is the smallest civic unit of collective doing in this model of existence. Polynesian cultures have had to evolve, survive, and thrive in the eye of some of nature's most climactic and catastrophic events—and to do that demands more than just relentless commitment; it requires the capacity for high performance against all odds. The volatility of this environmental truth also creates a foundation for compassion. The selfish gene at work in Hawaiian culture would have rendered itself extinct long ago. Evolution would have soon discarded it as not fit for purpose. The Hawaiian culture has of necessity been predicated on a mutual sense of care for each other—the compassionate undertaking of belonging and coexistence in the eye of nature's greatest power and might. Looking at the storm clouds and mists gathering around the peaks towering over the Hanalei River, the truth of things greater than oneself reasserts itself to anyone who might choose to forget it. And humility demands compassion. If we are all in some way vulnerable or wanting, we all deserve compassion.

High-performing individuals with a compassionate and caring nature, in whichever tasks they choose to act in the world, are the foundation of *'ohana* and Hawaiian resilience. This is well worth considering at greater length, regardless of where we live or with whom.

A Simple Exercise in Working Your Empathy

When you exercise, it is worth remembering what effect that performance-enhancing activity is having on *all* aspects of the heart, not just the physical. The next time you are exercising and you start to feel your skin buzzing and the endorphin rush hitting, try to picture not just the blood pumping through your veins but the electromagnetic field around your heart lighting up. Picture those 40,000 neurons firing. Imagine your autonomic system priming, switches being flicked, and your conscious self opening up and opening out. Imagine your EQ—your emotional quotient—sparking, going up three clicks; and then think about who or what you might point that electric conscious energy at. Performance and compassion are the engine room of our civilization and our exceptional existence—and at the center of that engine room? The human heart. Time to fire it up.

As with every exercise in this book, you can do this regardless of where you live, how much money you have, and what job you do. You don't need a mountain to scale, an ocean to swim, or a river to run in order to exercise your EQ.

You just need you, your heart, and a compassionate purpose. One way to do this is to marry two tasks—one physical, one emotional—into a single exercise, and set yourself to it. Think of someone you really like or whose company you enjoy—someone who lives within a few miles of you. Think of that person. And then do two things. First, plot a course from your home to theirs: and second, choose your mode of transport. Just one condition: you may not involve planes, trains, or automobiles—or motorbikes, for that matter. Any mechanized transport is out. You can use a bike, skateboard, scooter, or your own two legs, either running or walking. The simple task? Undertake the journey between your home and theirs once a week for a minimum of four weeks; and challenge yourself to reduce the travel time by 10 percent every trip. Make the effort. Bathe in their company, heart open, senses on. Illuminate the journey home with a heart full of good stuff. And repeat. Exercising your empathy can be as simple as that.

BODY

If you have anything that makes the organism stronger,
smarter, healthier, it's going to influence everything.
All aspects of your life.
The whole.

—LAIRD HAMILTON

TO Laird, we are an amazing organism capable of realizing
so much more, both in ourselves and in our connection with
the world around us. He is less about reaching up toward some
higher being that we might aspire to be, and more about reaching back into the brilliant creature we already are.

In an age where AI and machine learning consume both our
thoughts and, increasingly, our jobs, fully comprehending what
it means to be human—and understanding how astonishing we
are as an organism—is becoming more and more of a priority.

Questions of machine-enabled immortality and the pursuit
of youth pervade our society and our culture.

We are now seeking to transform ourselves from the creature we are into a creature we dream of being; and yet we remain

uncertain as to whether that dream will ultimately make for a desirable reality and meaningful existence.

What it is to be human still seems to evade us.

We are dislocating ourselves from the creature we are, and from the natural world in which we have spent 100,000 generations evolving, without truly understanding what it is we are dislocating from.

In this chapter, Laird explores the raw materials of the creature we are, and how we connect with ourselves and to the world around us. He explores ideas and evidence of how we got here, what our existence means for us right now, what we're presently capable of, and what wonders may yet be revealed, if we only just bothered to try.

> Shigeru Miyagawa, a linguist at Massachusetts Institute of Technology, suggests that, between 50,000 and 80,000 years ago, humans merged the expressive songs of birds with the information-bearing communications of other primates to create the unique music that is human language.
>
> —JAY GRIFFITHS, "BIRDSONG"

LAIRD

I did a talk at a little elementary school. I asked the kids: "Write down what the greatest machine that you know is. What would your dream machine be? What would be the greatest machine that you could own?"

And some of them said airplane and race car and all

these different things, and I said, "Actually, you already own the greatest machine. It's your body. It's an amazing thing. It can fly. It can swim. It can run—it can do everything it can do. And any machine that you want to own or dream of owning—it can operate that machine as well."

We already possess the greatest machine. This vessel— this thing that carries all the cargo of us—it's a tool that you can shape, hone, and upgrade. You can make it a little faster, a little stronger, a little smarter.

If you nurture it, you can get a lot more out of it. Its capacity and its capabilities are amazing. It operates in silence, unsupported. It runs itself. No plugs. No processors. Feed it food and it has an energy source that it processes more efficiently than most other creatures—and under greater duress. It can heal your wounds time and again. It can withstand the extremes of altitude and depth—it absorbs pressures and forces that many other creatures can't. It can process poisons. It can regenerate itself.

And, given half a chance, it could be even more amazing still. Every day there are guys out there proving that the further we push the organism, the more the organism becomes capable of—all by itself. Forget the super-processed bolt-ons. The computational stuff. I'm talking at an organism level here.

And the only thing getting in the way of it doing more, being more? Us.

If we want to evolve, at an organism level, we've got to learn to get out of our own way. We've got to learn to stop putting bad stuff in our own way.

We've put some great stuff in our way. Shelter. Heat. Food. Clothing. Language. Mechanization. Technology. And look where it's taken us—it's amazing.

But we've got to pay a price. There's a trade in there. And I think we're starting to get an idea of the price of that trade now.

So, maybe reaching back into it. Stripping stuff back. Uncluttering it. Exploring it. That's an adventure right there.

In that sense, I think my relationship with my body is pretty open.

Part of it is being naked all the time. I wear shorts and that's all, pretty much—unless I go snowboarding where I've got to have a little bit of protection. I spend a good majority of my life either in surf shorts—fancy underwear—no shoes, no shirt—and most of that time I'm in the water.

So my sensitivity to environment through my body—and my durability in regard to pain due to generally being more exposed, more vulnerable—to the cut toe, or a surfboard spear—gives me a much stronger relationship with my body.

I'm a firm believer in the pleasure principle. Pleasure and pain (or discomfort) need each other. One can't exist without the other. You've got to be open to both of those experiences. The equal experience of them is what makes the whole. Kind of easy for me because I'm more exposed, and more likely to have both kick in at some point, sometimes simultaneously, sometimes in some kind of succession.

When the body is subjected to a certain experience, it acts as the conduit for all the things that brings. And if we're open to them, and don't hide from them, they are productive.

They're good. Doesn't matter which. Any pleasure, any pain—they're like a power charge to the body and we learn from them.

You receive everything through your body, through the

senses—your joy, your instinct, your pleasures, your pain—everything goes through the conduit of the body. So the simple logic is that the more in touch you are with it—then the better and more productive a relationship you'll have with all those experiences; all those feelings.

My search for understanding is less "big picture" and more about understanding the vessel. I put a priority on understanding—getting knowledge that's helpful to the body or just for all-around wellness, the condition of the organism.

My ears are always open. I'm always open and listening. And I try and make sure that I'm just around other people that are into it too, seeking understanding perhaps, in a similar way to me. But I don't just want a whole load of "Lairds" all sitting around going "Gee-whiz, didja know . . ." That would be real boring.

So between Gabby and I, our friends, and our XPTers, we're all seeking stuff and sharing it. Sharing is a big part of this. That's generosity right there. There's no selfish hiding "the" book or "the" specialist—to own it. We're like, "Hey, did you see this book, did you see this thing, here's a podcast on this, is that what you're referring to?"

All of us are seeking information, right? And there is a reward in that. I'm a big fan of intuition. Your instinct is there for a reason. Trust it. But that doesn't mean lock it in a tower. It's a muscle. It needs feeding. Updating. It needs an upgrade every so often. And it needs to be proven out.

And a lot of the time when you're open to that, the majority of scientific studies just confirm your intuition.

All those times when I've said, "Hey, I get this sensation" or "I feel *this*" or "I think *this* happens," I believe that a lot of what I intuit will eventually be explained by science. However crazy what I "feel" might seem, I believe that there will be certain scientific protocols that will eventually explain it. There will be a mathematical equation for that feeling—or an empirical piece of data that proves it.

So we've got to think about intuition as part of the interface—part of the interface between us and the organism. There's a lot of highly complex processes going on in there, some of which are still way beyond our wildest imagining. However advanced or mind-blowing you think human science may have got, it's way at the beginning on some of this stuff.

Your intuition is the interface between you and all that complexity. Your intuition is sitting there between your conscious and unconscious self. Just because you can't see it or it seems rooted in your subconscious somewhere, or just at the edge of your consciousness, doesn't make it voodoo.

Our body has spent a whole lot of time—thousands of generations—checking stuff out; watching, responding, reacting, adapting as we acclimated ourselves to new environments, dealing with new risks and threats. Testing. Cause and effect. Action. Consequence. Assess. Repeat. Improve. That's evolution right there. And your intuition is a big part of that—and of how you continue to navigate that.

That's what makes us brilliant. That's what makes us pretty damn amazing as creatures. That's the light switched on. Conscious and unconscious. The interface between us and the science of us.

So when you feel stuff, something, anything, and then later you get the data—the formal information or evidence—a lot of the time that data will just confirm your intuition.

So trust your intuition. But don't be confined by it. Test it. Feed it. Exercise it.

I'm always open to learning, and I never think in absolutes. Because you can bet your ass that when someone says, "Hey, this is the way and it's over here. This is the answer," that answer will just lead to a bigger question; and their answer will get put in the junk folder along with all the other billions upon billions of discarded answers and absolutes we've left along the evolutionary trail.

I'm always open to anything, and I like to test myself and be a guinea pig. I like to subject myself to other people's experiences, and have my own experiences too. I like to be a lab rat. I want to go try stuff out. New stuff. Right now, an example is my new protocol with my sauna, inspired by a podcast someone shared with me. The podcast focused on how saunas, far more than ice baths, help the body repair after strenuous exercise and injury in the way they compel the body to release heat-shock proteins. Firing up growth hormones. Stimulating and stressing the organism in ways that help it to repair. The same theory of extreme temperature as with ice, but a whole new set of good stuff.

So I'm going to stop my current training, the usual ice protocol, and I'm going to go, "OK, right now I'm going to do *this*": hot boxing, short periods at really high temperatures in the sauna, like at 220 degrees; then longer at lower; then longer and higher, whatever the variations are—and see what the effect is of it, on me, on my stamina, my repair timeframes—and then, depending on the legitimacy or not of that exploration—that will determine whether it becomes part of my life protocol. And I'm not assuming anything.

If it is important enough—if it has a big enough effect—I'll be like, "Yeah, that's proof. That's real."

Like right now I'm post–hip replacement, so I can test the edges of its ability to improve repair meaningfully. That's the deal. Test it. Prove it. Then you can use it knowingly.

With proof, I'll be prepared to say to the people I train and mentor, "Oh yeah, that's cool—you do that—it's great for recovery, and you can use it where you have an injury." And I can mean it.

It's the same way with all injury or post-workout repair, where you are continuously stressing the system, stressing the body. You're seeking a better way—a way that becomes a formula technique where you can go, "There's a certain thing you can do to get better faster."

It becomes part of your lifestyle. You apply it like everything else. "OK, I'm going to sleep and I'm going to eat well and I'm going to work out and OK, now, I'm going to hot box, I'm going to sauna before and after every workout. It's no different to what you normally do in your everyday life—with food, with knowledge. You're trying to nurture the system; but in this case it might be heightened and more exaggerated, because you're looking for recovery and repair and trying to really push the body in the way that it's designed to be pushed.

And the body responds to this stuff, because it's what we're built to do. It's how evolution designed us. That's why I'm a guinea pig. We're designed to be stressed in certain ways. That's why, at our best, we are so adaptable and efficient. That's what resilience is. But we've grown out of the habit.

"When it comes to the sauna and we're asked, *how do you think this works,* it probably does on a lot of levels— but probably the most profound one is that we are all in the same room within six feet of each other, and there's no technology here, and we're hanging out for the next thirty minutes talking—which probably hasn't happened for you all day."

—KELLY STARRET, CROSSFIT FOUNDER

I always use the analogy of water, because we are mostly made of water. And water always looks for the path of least resistance—always, no matter where you put it. It might go over there, only to come back the other way so that it can avoid any resistance.

And I think we have a built-in thing, in that we always look for the path of least resistance.

Whenever it's cold, we want heat. When it's hot, we want cold. And we always want to know how long the run's going to be. *How far are we going to run today? How far are we going right now?* Because I want to know—because my body wants to know—I want to know how to pace myself.

I'll always tweak Gabby because I'll never be specific. It drives her nuts.

"We're going for a bike ride."

"Well, where are we going?"

"I don't know."

"How far's it gonna be?"

"I'm not sure."

Because I'm not! I'm not going to be able to ride indefinitely—but I like to always put the unknown in there somewhere. That's where indistinct goals are really valuable; that's what they offer you. The benefit is in the not-knowing. The body can't adapt—it can't modify—it has to keep recalibrating, rebalancing, in flow. That's good stress, right there. Just by not saying, "Hey, its three miles long, or two thousand meters up, or one thousand strokes wide."

If you lift weights, and you keep adding weight to create resistance, that's fine. But you develop techniques in certain things, and if you did the same routine over and over and over, even with the increasing weight, you would be getting less and less from it.

Like with everything we do—you run every day, you run two miles; then you got to run three miles; then you got to run ten miles—pretty soon, it doesn't matter how far you run. You don't keep getting what you got out of the first one that you ran, or the second one that you ran, because you just become efficient, quickly. The body is smart and it looks for a million different ways to decrease the impact, because it wants to avoid expending energy.

The body seeks efficiency—it wants to put as little energy into the process as it possibly can. That's how it has been designed. That's what our relentless evolution has brought to us. That's part of survival—becoming more efficient—so we're going to put in the least amount of energy to get from A to B.

By the hundredth time, the thousandth time, whatever it is you're doing, you're going to be so efficient at it that you can do it with your eyes shut, backwards, with your hands tied behind your back.

So I seek out new things because I think that new things have a tendency to stress us pretty easily, in a way that's good for us, in a way that improves us.

"In XPT we don't want the shortcuts; we want the long way 'round. And there's a real point to that; of being present in the experience. That's the gift I get. I start to love life, I love those moments, there's so much for me personally. When you're in the movie business like I am, then almost every encounter turns into 'What can I get you to do for me?' This is different. I feel like I've got friends. You're pretty much naked with that group and there's not a way to hide, physically; emotionally; spiritually; any way."

—RANDALL WALLACE

First of all, with something new, you have no existing knowledge—so you don't have the shortcuts. You can't just apply an efficiency strategy just yet. You might be able to implement trying something new using skills you already have—because it's going to bring you to a new barrier. You're going to get these bigger rewards.

We look at the learning curve, and all of the big rise in the learning is early on. That's why making sure that you're always being a student, a novice—a beginner in something, anything—is so good for us. It goes back to the tools and strategies we use for retaining our youthful enthusiasm—for retaining that wonder you had as a kid. "Hey, let's try this—that's cool!"

In that ability to wonder and be curious, I think that's where we have the greatest rewards. I think wonderment is a muscle you should exercise every day. That's a skill; that willingness to subject yourself to things you haven't done—not worrying about what people think. Worrying if you're no good at stuff, or you goof off.

I spent a career doing shit where people just go, "What are you doing? That's stupid. Why is that guy doing that?" And I would just ignore them and just do it—and five or ten years later, I'm watching them do it and I'm laughing—and I'm going, "Yeah, pretty dumb, isn't it—but how *good* is that?!"

But it's less about that—about the fact that if you just experiment, do your own thing, eventually people come 'round. It is more about that willingness to subject yourself to being that beginner. Because you're going to go through the pain and suffering of it. You're going to fall on your ass. You are going to humiliate yourself. Period.

So you have to motivate yourself. And anyone around you. Because this stuff is infectious. Being a novice. Being a beginner is infectious. It's fun.

You're released from having to always "know," to have the answer. Not always having the moves, the chops, the perfect arc, the perfect ride. That's good for us. As people. As a species.

As a species, we could do with not knowing the answer all the time.

But the big deal is that we learn. We evolve when we try new things. I said to someone recently who doesn't really do the snow thing, "Go learn how to snowboard and see how sore and tired you are the first day, and the second day, and the third day—how you just feel like somebody beat you with a bat."

But if you've been snowboarding a long time, you can snowboard all day almost every day and you will evolve less and less; learn less and less.

Only human beings have the capacity for controlled, systematic, foresighted, hypothesis-testing curiosity.

—DANIEL C. DENNETT, *FROM BACTERIA TO BACH AND BACK*

So try something new. Something that you suck at. I think that the continued stressing of the system is where we really excel. The body loves to do that—the neurons are firing—trying to create new neuron pathways to create improved motor-skill technique. When all these things are happening, that is when we're in the greatest part of our growth and the best part of our trajectory.

I've been surfing for so long, another day out surfing is probably not going to make me get better. It's going to be hard to have any effect. One day on top of thirty, forty, or fifty thousand hours is not going to do anything.

But me doing something new—stressing the body in such a way as to have some breakthrough in my endurance, or my flexibility, or my mental strength? That could have a huge effect on my performance on the water. I could do something not directly connected to surfing, have that breakthrough, and all of a sudden, *boom*, you just have this different gear; you're routing the information in your brain a different way, and you've indirectly impacted on something you thought was at the end of its curve in improvement terms.

I mean, a really simple example is music. Music can be performance-enhancing. I can be deep-sand running, whatever, and, because the music is occupying a certain channel in me, the information that it takes to actually do the activity is rerouted through a different channel, which potentially opens up some new doors.

But in all of this, in trying new things, in stressing the body, its ability to economize is amazing. And it's not always the least-resistance kind—the evasion form—of economy.

Sometimes its efficiency mechanisms can be transformative—as with illness, or injury. I've experienced this myself. Some of the greatest performances occur when athletes are hurt or wounded.

Why? Well, maybe the body's like, *Hey, I don't have enough energy to do it wrong. I've got to do it exactly right with the minimal amount of effort—and I know this and this and this will do that—they will get me there with no waste.*

So why do I try a new sauna regime, or anything else? I don't know. At its simplest level, I'm looking for transformation. Maybe the hormonal change and the things that happen to my body from doing back-to-back saunas for three weeks straight could have an effect on me when I go have my season—an effect that could be really profound. So why would I not try? Why would I not try new things?

"Laird carries this physical energy and ability to concentrate—I mean, how much can you fucking train? Because this is the guy who wants to wake up and go. He wants to wake up and react to what the day's meant to give him—and when it's the same all the time, it's like his version of hell."

—GABBY REECE

There's a whole lot of stuff that evolution has put in your tank. And we are barely touching the sides of it.

If the earth is charged with an energy, well, how much

greater is this ocean charged with an energy? And do we feel that, being in the water?

There are some specific biological effects that happen to the system just being in the water alone. The effect on the body, and the way it responds to just the pressurization of the water, it's like a light switching on.

The term *Master Switch of Life* . . . refers to a variety of physiological reflexes in the brain, lungs, and heart, among other organs, that are triggered the second we put our faces in water. The deeper we dive, the more pronounced the reflexes become, eventually spurring a physical transformation.

—JAMES NESTOR, *DEEP*

Consider how much stuff you absorb through your skin. When you're in seawater you're in rich company: seawater is alive, with energy, nutrients, life forms. You're in the water and your skin is absorbing stuff. There is a transfer of chemicals, of energy, happening between you and the ocean.

You can feel and you can experience it, and I think that's one of the things that draw us to be in the ocean. It's more than just the pleasure of riding a wave, or the beauty of paddling your board or sailing, whatever.

I think there's something deeper that calls us to go— and part of that can be that it's the place that we've come from. I mean, all life comes from the ocean. There's an old understanding at work there. Time moves differently there. And we have evolved to embrace that.

When you understand that the unconscious mind moves

thirty-two times the speed of the conscious mind—then you start to realize what that organism of yours is capable of; it's like hey, you can have superpowers. As far as your conscious mind is concerned, your unconscious mind is seeing the future.

Our ability to sense things and tap into what could be considered almost superhuman capabilities—where we have some kind of X-Men-type potential—is not as crazy as it sounds. It's not just like one day you wake up and all of a sudden you can shoot light-rays out of your eyeballs. It's the process of becoming aware and then having that stuff slowly affect you.

I sometimes wonder whether the potential to have that level of connectedness, that kind of understanding that would allow us the comfort of not having to continue searching—maybe reconnecting with that stuff would remove our need for mystery, for some metaphysical truth.

We would be OK with just being here. The whales and the dolphins—they're cool with eating, mating; having their families and playing in the water—the existence of just being alive. Maybe the part of it we come into contact with through the primitive thing allows us a certain ability to be content. Perhaps primitivism is an exercise in contentment.

Whether it's in meditation or in an active meditative form like exercise or sport, we're searching for these answers: Why? Who? Where? What?

In my own personal experience, active meditation; being out there, looking beyond my limitations, reaching; that's my connection mechanism. I don't get too lost in the philosophical guru space. I don't have some "special" secret thing. For me it has nothing to do with that, it just has to do with your own well-being as a human.

THE FILLING STATION. This is it. The heart of my 'ohana. My jet fuel. My power source. My reason for being. Fill up on feeling and everything is possible. If I ever forget why I do what I do, they're there to set me straight.

NURTURE NATURE. Tending to what's precious to us is critical. If we don't care for what surrounds us—our family, our people, our community and environment—who the hell else will? We have to be able to trust each other to care.

ICE AGE. It's hard to explain the feeling of being in ice. It's timeless—beyond explanation. You've just got to do it. Go to the store. Buy bag loads of it. Put it in the bath. And try it—immerse yourself. Your body will thank you for it.

UNDER PRESSURE. Hydrostatic workouts are the best. Get into water. Test your stamina. Stress your breath. Feel the organism talk to you. And, more important, listen and reciprocate. This is a two-way street.

EVERYTHING IS CONNECTED. Up through the water into the core of the body. Across it through your fascia. From the outside in, through the skin and senses. Sound. Pressure. Balance. Temperature. Tension. Friction. Gravity. Momentum. Enjoy it.

THE LIP OF LIFE. Sometimes you get to the top of your wave and you can see everything. Sometimes all you see is the next wave. And sometimes you just see someone cutting across your line. That's life. Be OK with it.

GOOD FAIL. Getting things wrong is the fastest way to learn. That's how we evolve. Playing at the edges of what we're capable of. Stressing and testing. If I'm not falling into, onto, out of, or off of something, I'm not trying hard enough.

WHAT GOES UP . . .
The art is not in how you scale the heights. The art is in how you come down. Because there is always going to be a "down" somewhere in life. So when it happens: deep breath, heart wide open, senses on, and go.

STONE LOVE.
Don't pump weights. Move rocks—physically, intellectually, spiritually. We're designed to move, think, feel in ways that are useful. Train to be useful, not to be pumped or ripped.

MIND OVER MATTER. If your feet are the great connectors, imagine what getting your brain close to the earth can do. All that electromagnetic exchange, circulatory testing, core stressing, and of course, a different view.

87% PERFECT. We're all flawed. It's how we're made. It's just about balance. I love and want to protect the ocean. But I also love gunning a Jet Ski across it. Should or could I be paddle boarding? Sure. But this is a lot of fun.

KLINGON. The planet we're on is spinning in space at 1,037 miles per hour with 1g of gravity pulling on us. What looks unnatural to us is sometimes the most natural thing we can do. Free your mind and everything will follow.

JUNK DNA. Everything in this shed serves a purpose. It all has a use. Even the stuff that hasn't been fully used in months or years is tended to, serviced, and fully functioning. Everything here is a small piece of what shaped me.

SWEET SWEAT. Sweating is more than just a temperature regulatory system. It's like a spring-clean and a jump-start rolled into one. Extreme heat has been used for millennia for "cleansing" ourselves both physically and spiritually.

SHOWER POWER. Used as part of a hot and cold regimen, you can't beat the shower. A short hit on cold in the morning? That'll kick the system in, tighten your fascia, and clear your mind. That's total clarity right there.

DRAG KING. Heavy is what you make it. I'd rather drag logs and sleepers than lift weights. Period. The twist and turn of this stuff works my fascia in a way two more stacks on a barbell never could. And work rate is everything.

I think right now, in a world that's getting a whole lot faster through technology, we need to really know and understand what it is to be human.

There's a whole load of folks worrying about some futuristic robot-ruled planet. More realistically, we have AI and supercomputing, and a whole lot of folks quietly worrying about their jobs.

But I don't think we're ever going to get completely away from being human, because that's what we are. Sci-fi and cyborgs and other stuff aside, we're never going to not be human.

I think that greater connectedness to the organism we are could definitely help us to seek and to have an understanding of what it is to be human; an understanding that will make us calmer—that will calm us down and maybe affect our values and other spiritual aspects. Balance some of this extreme stuff out.

Maybe in stressing the organism, stressing the body, and in unlocking this stuff in ourselves, that is what we're going to find through that door. Something that begins to affect our spirituality and our well-being.

Whatever you think about spirituality, or connectedness, or religion, or whatever you want to call it, a belief system of some sort is obviously playing some kind of role in our evolution—it's obviously mandatory—because we have it.

And that means that it's useful. Evolution is smarter than us. We don't have things in our body that we don't need: we don't have mechanisms and motor skills that we don't need. We have language because it helps us to evolve. I don't think we would have belief systems if we didn't need them in some form and some way.

It must be a necessity for the equilibrium—the balance

that we need. A balance that we've kind of lost. Being in touch with the more primitive, animal side of us is as important as us going to a higher level of consciousness.

It is so important for us to be in touch with both. Reaching into the organism and throwing a few old switches—unlocking some of these things buried deep in our DNA and revealing a little more of our primal self—I think that's a part of how we create balance. I think we're a little too much *mind* these days.

It is inefficient for us to separate mind and body. We are lesser for it. Not better. One of the biggest mistakes we make is the separation between them. We create a separation: black and white; left and right; either/or. You're a jock or you're the smart guy.

But you have to nurture both. There's a relationship between intelligence and physicality. Some pretty smart guys in history knew that. You don't separate them.

With a few exceptions, the great geniuses of history were gifted with remarkable physical energy and aptitude, none more so than Da Vinci.

Leonardo's extraordinary physical gifts complemented his intellectual and artistic genius. . . . Leonardo was renowned for his poise, grace, and athleticism. . . . And his strength was legendary. . . .

Dr. Kenneth Keele, author of "Leonardo da Vinci. The Anatomist," refers to him as "a unique genetic mutation."

—MICHAEL J. GELB,

HOW TO THINK LIKE LEONARDO DA VINCI

Intelligence is a remarkable thing. But that's not all of it. The intelligence that our conscious self has pursued is very new. There's a whole load we don't know. And perhaps never will.

That's why we will continue to strive. If we knew everything, then what would we do? We need mystery—we need that, and that's actually to our benefit. There's got to be some reason for how complex life is.

In the end, us not knowing is probably essential—because knowing *too* much isn't healthy. You see what it does. It's not exactly always productive. It does have some of the answers, but not always—not in pure evolutionary terms for us as humans.

If humans need to evolve their humanity, what's a numbers game got to do with the emotional side—or the spiritual? You know, for example, in chess, in a man-versus-supercomputers situation, supercomputers are going to win, right? It's a calculation game. It's just numbers and probability. OK, so the machine beats the chess master—but what does that have to do with feelings?

The machine is not conscious as we know it. They're trying to create conscious machines—but we're here. We're already it. But we're just an old-fashioned human machine, right—and that's flawed. And we don't like flawed anymore. We don't like old. We don't do wisdom. That's out the window.

You know it's all connected. Our search for super-knowledge. To know all things. To override death. Human death. We're looking for an override switch. We can't deal with the fact that we're an organism and so we'll die. But you know, that's the price for being us. For being able to do and feel everything we do. You don't get that forever.

And through our bodies, right, these amazing vessels we kick about in, we are connected to the world about us in ways science cannot even comprehend yet. Connectedness is in our DNA.

In 1984 Edward O. Wilson, a Harvard University biologist, naturalist, and entomologist, coined the term "biophilia" to describe his hypothesis that humans have "ingrained" in our genes an instinctive bond with nature and the living organisms we share our planet with. He theorized that because we have spent most of our evolutionary history—three million years and 100 thousand generations or more—in nature (before we started living in communities and building cities), we have an innate love of natural settings.

—WALLACE J NICHOLS,
BLUE MIND

The organism is an amazing thing. Take your feet. That wouldn't be a place to put a nerve ending, let alone a load of them, right? Evolution wouldn't put them there unless there was a specific reason. That wouldn't be a place to put nerve endings that connect to every major organ in our bodies— unless it was an efficient or effective thing to do.

That's the basis of reflexology—the whole thing is based on the fact that we can use pressure on our feet to influence the organs in our body. So that tells you that our feet have been designed to work that way.

Our feet are the external remote for our internal organs. They have a job to do. We're meant to be absorbing energy from the earth as we walk around, energy that can affect our inner health—or at least we did before shoes got in the way.

This is everyday stuff, right? You don't need to be hot-footing over a volcanic island to get the benefits of this. Or even standing and balancing on golf balls. Just taking your shoes off more often. Stand in the garden. Walk over some gravel in the drive. That's a beginning. You can wake your feet up in real easy ways.

There's clues everywhere to our evolutionary journey. Clues to all of the stages we've evolved through. Look at the stages human embryos go through. That's our journey right there. It's no surprise. When I broke my collarbone—my doctor goes, "Don't worry about that [collarbone]. That was just a leftover from when we had wings."

But my theories aren't always palatable to everyone.

For example, I always have a debate about sunscreen—and people are always saying, "You don't use sunscreen . . . that's bad."

Well, maybe. But I believe that my skin's designed to absorb the sun. Same with my eyes. I don't wear sunglasses because I believe that my eyes can handle the light that's created by the sun. So we make our choices. And mine are based on my belief that we are part of the natural world and we're designed for it. One of my favorite lines is:

"We are it. And it is us."

I think sometimes there's a disconnect. We're the first culture in the history of man that fears the sun. Every other culture throughout history has always worshipped the sun. We're the first one that's covering up and getting sunscreen on. We have developed an innate fear of it.

People sometimes forget that without sun, there's no life. Yes, there are problems with skin cancers developing, the rate of them, but equally there are diseases that you get by not being in the sun enough.

That's just another example of a disconnect from our bodies and the relationship to the environment—to the world. Our bodies know what to do with this stuff.

Hawaiians have a really clear idea about how all this joins up. How they act together with the universe. I suppose I have absorbed that. Sometimes unknowingly. But I must have done.

Growing up in a culture where physicality and warriors, and strength and skill, were rewarded and respected has obviously left its mark. In Hawaiian culture the best surfer was second only to the king or the chief.

Physicality was connected to survival: the purest purpose we have as an organism. Your skill in the ocean was connected to sources of life—food through fishing and surviving beyond the reef. Your ability to get beyond the reef, into the unknown, and come back. That was massive.

They talk in Peru about the guys who were surfing the reed boats three thousand years ago. You're a fisherman and the surf's up. Now, you can't *not* go out, just because the surf's up. You can't *not* go fishing. You've got to feed the village—everybody's got to eat.

So your ability to come in and out of the surf would inevitably make you understand how to catch a wave, would inevitably make you want to perfect that skill, because whoever was good at that would be able to go in and out of the surf, no matter what the surf was doing.

That skill would make you a very sought-after guy. So you're adapting to the environment—but it's got to be for a reason—and that reason used to be survival.

"What's interesting for me is, you go into the water with
Laird, and he looks different. He changes, instantly—
doesn't matter what he's doing—he could be body-
surfing, diving—but he changes—his face changes, the
way the body looks changes."

—GABBY REECE

Our bodies are the conduit to so much. They are connected to so much. And we've got a lot of the same DNA as
a lot of other creatures on the planet. So who knows what we
share. Who knows what we've got in the tank.

How does the whale find Hawaii again? They go to
Alaska and come back to Hawaii. How does a shark find its
way? Because they're still connected to the earth—they're
connecting into that primal thing.

Magnetoreception [is] an attunement to the magnetic
pulses of the Earth's molten core. Research suggests that
humans have this ability and likely used it to navigate
across the oceans and trackless deserts.

—JAMES NESTOR, *DEEP*

The Hawaiians once practiced this art called "flying." It
was an art of energy, obviously. Curiously, they would put
their testicles in the bottom of the canoe to navigate. Before they were navigating by the stars, they were using their
body to navigate. They *sensed* the direction. Intuited it. In

the same way the same people could sense illness in people too. They knew if somebody had something wrong.

But discuss the idea that my body might have the ability to actually navigate a magnetic line and everyone's like, *"Really?"*

So I think we really need to make up our mind here. The science speaks real clearly here. This isn't voodoo. Whales can do it, and a shark and the dolphin can do it—then why not a human? Why not? If we share so much of our DNA with whales and porpoises—why not?

In that way you could say we've regressed, not progressed, in a lot of it because we've numbed all of these abilities. Or just switched them off.

We need to spend more time reaching back into those more primitive capabilities, exploring. That's revelation right there. That's transformative.

And physicality is a big lever in all this. Take the whole thing about being in the Now—and using your physicality to do it. That makes more sense to me.

The mindfulness approach—developing some kind of learned skill that might take forever—I have friends that are really into that, into transcendental meditation, and they've been doing it for twenty years. But that doesn't do it for me. I'm just not built that way.

Stressing the body creates a Now. Your body, with some temperature shock, is placed there completely: right in the Now—to the point where you don't really need to have to think about anything. And for my meditative friends, when they've tried it they're like: "Wow, I went deeper than I ever have."

We have that ability built into us. It's just a matter of waking it up; and I think our ability to, you know, shock ourselves into it is a lot more efficient than to just try to "conscious" ourselves into it. The door to it is in our DNA. And that's the part that makes this inclusive, not exclusive. We've all got DNA. We've all got a pretty similar genetic imprint.

It's not like you have to go to the Himalayas or sit in a rock room for twenty years. You're going to be able to do this stuff immediately—because it's already programmed into us.

And it's transformative. Shamans and holy men have used the body—shocking the body—as a doorway to a heightened sense of everything for thousands upon thousands of years.

Getting more people to just use temperature shocking to turn it on—and feel that switch get switched—and go, "Wow! everything's on!"—is great, but we still need to remember to nurture it.

People don't go willingly to ice baths or hot boxes. Part of it is social training. We need a bunch of training to stop us acting like the water creature we mostly are, always looking to the path of least resistance.

We don't want to expose ourselves to the shocking cold. We came from that cold water—we had thousands and thousands of years in the cold. Sure, there was the odd thermal spring—and it's no surprise that those became spiritual places, places of transcendental experience—but getting and staying out of the cold has been a long and hard journey, and we're not going to let it go easily anytime soon.

And society teaches us that cold is bad. Everything is turned to that. *Catch a cold. Coldhearted.* It's in our language. These are all negative connotations, so whenever we're talking about cold, there's a negativity to it.

Warm is comfort: *I'm warm. I'm cozy. Put some warm clothes on. Turn the heating up.*

Warm is good and cold is always bad. So when I suggest shocking—extreme cold and heat—we already have a psychological thing that we're working against.

Again, the shocking and stressing of the body is not exclusive. This is not just for some surfer dude sitting on his board on the Pipeline waiting for Nirvana, or some superjock in a million-dollar training center.

This can be everyday stuff. Simple. At the end of your shower in the morning, try switching the shower to cold. And hold yourself there. Feel it across yourself. Over your head. Across your skin.

In a few short steps we can get our body from sleep to on and open—and it's not complicated.

Does all of this matter in the end—hot, cold, on, off, evolution, conscious, unconscious? I think so. As creatures, however brilliant we are, we need help here, even in the smallest things—now more than ever.

Everyone expects so much—and feels so entitled to so much—and yet fails in the making of it. There is an enormous amount of physical and emotional and social insecurity in people—and anxiety.

And everything we're putting into our bodies is just making it worse—like some drinks out there. To me, as a purist, coconut water and all those new water-plus kinds of drink still have way too much additives and additions in there.

But baby steps, right? Would I judge someone for drinking coconut water? No way. Comparing Coke or Red Bull or whatever other stuff we're drinking to coconut water is like comparing some weird reconstituted meat burger, triple fries, and a full fat shake to a kale salad and no dressing.

If you're choosing to make even the smallest improvement, that's all good.

But we all need help, because it's confusing out there. We need help to navigate all that stuff. Choice has become a disease. We are overwhelmed by it to the point of it making us unwell.

The food stuff out there, the information, the directives, the fads; it's confusing. Margarine versus butter. Raw butter versus pasteurized butter. Sugar synthetics versus cane sugar. White rice. Brown rice. Vegetables good. Lectins bad. Fat plus sugar bad. Fat good? Good fats good.

No one is winning any prizes out there for making this stuff simple.

It's not surprising that people close off to the "experts." Each theory gets set up and then shot down. So people don't trust stuff anymore. Add to that the fact that some experts and scientists and nutritionists have been working for some corporations and sectors with a pretty dodgy rep in regards to their responsibility to the people they sell some of this shit to, and I'm surprised anyone listens to anyone, ever.

We need to simplify stuff. And we need to trust our intuition when doing so. We *know* when what we're eating or drinking is bad for us. We know. Our bodies know. It's whether we care. Whether we care enough. That's honesty.

Our ego and arrogance make us think, *Hey, I'm just great, thanks. I'm top of the food chain.*

I wonder whether we've created AI for more than just making shit get done faster by less people. That's our new predator right there. We killed off all the rest. And medicine is doing a pretty good job on the disease side of things. So perhaps that's us driving our own evolution. Killed all the predators—but we *need* predators to keep us on our toes. To keep all the switches on. So we made a new one.

Who knows. If we're going to throw in the towel—if we're just going to roll over and say, "Let the machines have it"—then, OK, don't bother.

But. Before we do that, I think the first thing we should do, all of us, is to know ourselves. Let's make sure we know what we're putting on the scrap heap, before we start worshipping the machine.

The real danger, I think, is not that machines more intelligent than we are will usurp our role as captains of our destinies, but that we will *over*-estimate the comprehension of our latest thinking tools, prematurely ceding authority to them far beyond their competence.

—DANIEL C. DENNETT,
FROM BACTERIA TO BACH AND BACK

We are amazing organisms—even in spite of ourselves.

Look at what we can endure. Look what the organism can endure. We can smoke cigarettes, drink whiskey, eat crap—live in a terrible state. All these toxins. We put our body through all of this shit and then we just give it any little bit of nurturing and it just excels. I mean our bodies are really durable.

I'd say it's almost more shocking that we're not getting more hammered, given what we've done—that we're not paying a greater price—and sooner. It's amazing. And I guess we could say that about the earth, too.

Back to that truth about nature. We are it. It is us.

I think we're "little earths." We're all little earths, and I think both the big earth and us little earths are in a pretty similar place. We're toxifying the vessel. We're polluting the vessel—ours and the planet's. The two are connected. And that's not a coincidence. Self-respect for ourselves and the planet we live on are connected. One affects the other.

If you look at nature—if you look at nature and how the creatures coexist with their environment—there is harmony. There's codependence. There's a natural respect.

But us, for the brilliant creature we are, with all of this evolution, with all of our consciousness, with all the amazing things we can do, we still seem to just screw this stuff up.

But you know, just like we are with all that stuff inside us, out of sight is out of mind. And mind is everything for us as a species at the moment. In the same way that we ignore or dismiss all of those aspects inside of us and programmed into us, part of us through evolution—it's the same with the environment around us, the natural world that our body's capabilities and intuitions are connected to and a part of.

To be aware of the unseen. To respect and be responsive to it. That's the gift we can give ourselves right there. But we're just like, *The what? The where?*

But hey: Deforestation? Acidification of the ocean? Plastic pollutants? *Not my problem. Not in my world. Can't see it. Don't care.* It either isn't important or it doesn't exist.

There's the problem with us and the unseen right there. We lack the imagination to embrace it.

BAREFOOT BUSINESS

Body & the power of a strong culture

The culture of a business is central to world-class performance. It is what threads the business together, builds its resilience and energy from the inside out and the ground up.

Purposeful businesses and businesspeople, seeking to build a culture around both making money and doing good, reap measurable rewards.

Every company listed on the *Firms of Endearment* website runs a very visible cultural program.

These Firms of Endearment outperform the S&P 500 at scale over time.

The campus cultures of leading businesses are testimony to culture being paramount in the development and innovative capability of disruptive and sector-defining businesses.

A strong, engaging, and meaningful culture is what strengthens the corpus of any business, from two people to twenty to two thousand.

Businesses that use culture to create a sense of family and belonging are not only businesses to be reckoned with, but businesses that are to be admired—and imitated. Because they are the strongest threads weaving through a healthy and resilient business landscape, vital to its balance and well-being.

Here, Laird and Gabby talk about how their relationships with people in every business they run—from the most incidental interactions to the most central partnerships—are key to their success. They also explore their concept of what makes a good business.

LAIRD

At the end of the day, I think it's essential that you care. That you care no matter what.

If you care, sincerely and deeply, people can feel that. But, equally, there are many in business who feel that when you care, you're going to create that kind of relationship a lot of people don't want, or value.

They don't want the responsibility that a true duty of care might bring. Because they're scared. Because if you care, that makes you vulnerable.

So I think most people would like to avoid caring. It's like the sea. They don't look at the coral on the bottom. Out of sight, out of mind. One less thing to worry about. They don't think of tending to even the smallest part.

So I think that caring about your business as a whole, and caring about the people themselves individually, sincerely; I think that creates culture—a powerful culture.

For a leader, whether you're an officer or you're a priest, or a teacher or a community leader, it's all about caring. And caring is powerful. Compassion and a sense of duty of care is powerful. It certainly worked for Jesus, for Buddha, for Martin Luther King, for Gandhi—and anybody who's been a leader of the light.

Even now, it's a struggle for some businesspeople to talk about social compassion and awareness—or community. They think you're not being serious about business if you lead on that.

People misconceive being compassionate and caring as weakness. But you know, compassion? That's true power—when you're in a position to go, "Hey—it's about service.

It's not about taking; it's about giving." Then all of a sudden that's when you really gain.

That's where I think the difference between small, owner-run businesses and publically traded businesses lies.

The profit margins drive a disconnect of care—and the focus and ethos become different. They become different beasts, you know. Then there's something else that really no one has any connection to—that results in all kinds of weird decisions that aren't necessarily good for humanity.

But being uncaring doesn't get them anywhere, ultimately. And then they start to lose success, too—it ends up hurting their success.

You see the retreat from profit sometimes—where they get the founders back to help make it survive after the MBAs get in there and number it to death.

It happened at Nike; somebody got in there and decided they didn't need athletes anymore—they were just going to sell the products with the products.

That got Phil Knight right out of his bed, and he kept running back in there to put stuff straight: "No, we are our people—that is our business."

That's why it's a lot more common now, when these younger businesses are being bought up by these bigger ones, they retain everybody. The bigger businesses are learning. They leave all the guys in the business.

They're learning that if you start to affect the quality of care and the quality of the image, and the culture, and the quality of the product—that affects the value. You end up with a disproportionate relationship between what you are getting and what you are giving.

Part of the deal now is you're going to stay with the company for, you know, an extra four or five years or whatever—you've got to be in there in order to preserve quality.

If that was what was presented to me as an option? To have that as a choice? That would definitely drive me away, because that goes against all of my DNA.

Allowing chips to keep being knocked off the quality in the search of volume and margins? To make money? That makes no sense to me.

And the code you live by, and the kind of community you build, is not just about your own benefit.

Shared benefits are good. Businesses where everyone wins are a good thing.

That's how we've evolved. Collaborating, and then acting, together. And the benefits of doing that.

Maybe part of why you're running a business or businesses is because you're supporting a small group of people who are pivotal for no other reason than you just want them to be able to thrive and survive.

At that point you might consider sustaining a community quite profitably.

But for that to succeed, you have to be clear about specifically what the business is providing.

What is it providing? And is that what you want from it? Most of what's being driven businesswise is about money—and because it's always about money, then it's always about these other things that aren't necessarily what is important to someone who cares about people.

Some people see caring as a curse in business. I see it as a gift.

Laird is amazingly compassionate. He can be incredibly attentive. But he won't humor people. He's OK with making people feel uncomfortable.

If you really get down to it, he'll always show up—but he won't make you necessarily feel really comfortable. That's just him. Testing. Everything with Laird is about testing.

Maybe he'll make you guess. Will he? Won't he? But he will—and in that way the culture around Laird and around us is pretty straight down the line.

Are we really doing this? OK. Once it's on the books it's on the books—big or small—whether it's a phone interview or it's a major campaign.

It's all going to be treated the same. And yes, compassion is always there, and way more compassion than me by the way—way more.

I'm probably meaner that way than Laird ever is. That's our balance. That's our tension. But that's what makes you strong. That openness.

We've had situations small and large with XPT where it's like: "Problem—so OK, let's get on the phone."

And it doesn't even mean that you're always going to hang up the phone agreeing—but you're going to always come away with that mutual respect and some sense of solution for all the sides—and also the openness of going, "Hey listen, these are growing pains," or whatever.

So the culture around us is definitely a balance.

Laird will just go in and could just fire-hose everything—and I try and step back a little.

He's like, "You're very diplomatic and you go this way and that way," and I'll go, "Yeah, because you don't just come in and clear the decks."

But I really appreciate that about Laird. He'll just come in and be like, "This is bullshit"—but even when that happens (and there have been very few instances where it has), he still has a deep sense of caring for all of the people involved.

He's rough, he's gruff, he wants to surf; leave him alone. He wants to go to bed early and eat food. But he's actually not a mean person, and his care and attention is applied to everyone—it really is. It's *'ohana.*

Even when someone really screws up, he'll always say, "Let's give him a chance to make it work."

Because with as much ego as he has, to do what he needs to do, in a weird way he never gets his ego up too much.

But as I say, he doesn't sugarcoat stuff or put on an act. There is not an inauthentic bone in his body.

You'll see this when we do XPT stuff. If he's in a bad mood, he'll be in a bad mood—you'll get that—and he's not going to put on a smiley face for the sake of it—but he is really paying attention. A hundred and ten percent. But he isn't going to put a bow on it to make you feel better.

That's the culture. It's learning how you're doing with life, and improving yourself in true fitness but through other things as well—the culture you build around you, the community. Every single aspect of that business has to be authentic.

If you think about building culture from the ground up, creating it around a person, that person has to have those attributes, that pure authenticity. There's no better culture to have than that. But that raw honesty starts with the person.

If you asked him, "Are you an entrepreneur?" he might

say, "I guess I am," but he wouldn't sit there and go, "I'm a surfer, and I'm an entrepreneur." He would never say that. He would say, "I'm a waterman." It's straight. That's the heart of the culture right there. We both respect and value that.

The people we have in all these different businesses in their own right are all that way. And what is interesting is, as you are going through the hard times with these people, what keeps it going and progressing and growing is that underneath it all, you actually really respect each other; even in the times when you really don't agree. You don't ever go: "Fucking idiot."

The heavy corporate side of things doesn't do it for me. I get [that] the scale requires a certain framework or model of management and culture, but it makes you gray.

Entrepreneurship, with its risk and possibility, keeps you shiny—and that's the thing we like. We have this thing about shiny people versus matte people.

I would still rather travel through my life and try to be positive and shiny than be forced into some matte-gray life where I am protecting, hoarding, defending, and proving.

Enjoy it—and also hopefully enjoy the people you're working with—which for me is actually the number one priority. If you're actually enjoying each other and having fun, it barely gets better than that—and that's everything, right? To do it together is pretty magical.

For me that goes back to team sports, right? I know how much better I am with others; *I could do this on my own—or I could do this with you.* And that's always excited me—and I think that's been helpful in running these businesses. And Laird is pretty good about that, and I think, now that he's a little bit older, I feel he's more comfortable—he has carved out real estate for himself—so I think maybe that liberates him a little to just *be.*

For Laird—he has a different set of rules he's playing by. He understands that he can always trust himself to generate and manifest new things, even if he doesn't know what it is right now. And I think he's really comfortable with that. I don't think he's trying. I don't think he's like, "I got to go down to my shop and just really think of something new." I just think he's like, "I'm going to go on my path, and based on the way that I probably do things, whatever it is, it's going to show itself."

It's his mechanism. It's his true way of living and being. He's not going to try to be multiple things. He will just allow them to reveal themselves to him.

I think it's important that we can develop other dimensions—either I'm a CEO or I'm a mom, or I'm someone's wife; or I'm just a pretty young girl—but for me it's about defining the one thing you are *first.* Could you actually put all those various expectations and labels to one side for the moment, and be about something first that then lives in all those spaces?

People need to know that's OK too. You've got to follow yourself, and you have to do things for your own real reasons. That's him in business. It's that simple. It's like—buy the shit, like the shit, hate the shit; whatever it is—but do something with it. Make something of it.

Own It

Nature's been busy. And nowhere has she been busier than with that multitudinous herd of brilliant creatures we call the human race. Our genetic makeup clearly points to our connectivity to every living organism on this planet. Whether we like having banana and frog genes within us or not, they are there. An echo of our connectivity to everything. From the genetic truth of us outward, we are designed to be social. And if our genes have any say in the matter, that sociability should be nurtured at every opportunity. It should reach beyond the human self into the people we are inextricably connected to, and into the natural world we slithered, crawled, scuttled, and climbed out of.

Our most recent evolutionary path has imbued us with the faculty of consciousness, but for Laird this new faculty must not be at the cost of deserting the primal creature we are, or abdicating our responsibility to the natural world that formed us.

For Laird it is all too obvious that the veneer of our civilized self cracks and peels all too quickly when panic or fear sets in. Put simply, our civility deserts us under extreme duress. All that is left is the primal creature, honed over millennia to survive.

In Laird's view, we need to embrace the fact that in the brilliant creature we are, two selves reside: the chaotic, primal, survival-fixated self and the ordered, elevated, socially fixated self. And we must attend to both, as one.

We have perceptive trigger systems whose sole job is to relentlessly and tirelessly scan every ounce of information it can collect from our environment—movement, heat, sound, smell, light, air pressure, moisture, distance—process that information; and communicate it to us. Our primal senses then inform us of the potential outcomes of that processing, and adjust for them accordingly through simple and immediate actions. But we seem to spend most of our time trying to suppress these aspects of our primal selves. We need to connect to them, not disconnect from them.

One of the most potent frictions within Laird is that which exists between his absolute focus on the self—and the isolation that comes with connecting to what resides within him—and his absolute commitment to the community of souls among whom he lives: his social, civic sense of duty, born of his connection to people and the natural world. He denies no aspect of himself or of the culture and community that have shaped him. Quite the opposite. He *owns it*. Fiercely and without condition. Flaws, flakes, fuckups, and all.

It is from these two threads—**connection** and **community**—that we'll shape an example.

CONNECTION

Connection is a powerful thing. Not just in the sense of how everything fits together in the ecosystems of our bodies, lives, and societies—something we will explore more fully in the chapter "Everything Is Connected." For the moment, we are focusing on the simple blockchain of genetic truths that secure and underwrite our integrity as a species. These days, unless we choose to explore them through DNA testing and genetic sequencing, our genetic predispositions usually play little or no role in our conscious lives. Progress is a beautiful endeavor, but there are some by-products of our advancing civilization that affect our ability to remain connected to all that has gone before us. When we pursue innovation with such fierceness, we run the danger of losing a part of ourselves—especially that which celebrates a more ancient connectedness to all things. There is perhaps a genetic logic in why more ancient cultures, like that of Hawaii, call on their ancestors. They are simply invoking a genetic superiority—the capacity for survival and ability to prevail. For every one of those ancestors that stayed alive, and carved a life that resulted in children—who in turn did the same, all the way down to you—there is a genetic echo, something learned along the way, that is in your code—a proven strand of super-resilience. That is the kind of connection that we would do best not to take lightly.

COMMUNITY

"Community" has to be the most overused and misunderstood word trending on any current digital platform. Digital communities have rendered the borders of countries porous, and in some instances almost meaningless. But these communities would struggle to operate in a realm that Laird would both recognize and, more importantly, value. In Laird's eyes, real community is where people are stitched into each other's lives in the most banal and mundane ways, through multiple repetitive acts of shared existence—a mass of interdependent, integrated actions or micro-moments undertaken collectively in real time, in the real world, by real people. This cannot be replicated with the same passion and purpose in the digital world, for one simple reason: We are creatures. And we need intimacy and understanding to function optimally. For communities to survive over millennia requires that each individual's ability and desire to act for the collective good be *innate*—that it come as second nature. This cannot be achieved remotely or dispassionately, as Laird points out. You have to care. It is part of your role as a social creature, and to deny it is to lose a little of what made us brilliant creatures in the first place. For us to truly embrace this ethos, humility needs to be at work within us. Rationally, you could describe "community" as a simple piece of math— *real community = positive social interactions x number of people ÷ physical proximity.* Apply this simple equation, and your communal whole will always be greater than the sum of its individual human parts—a living, breathing, collaborative, caring community—not just another set of social network data points.

'Ohana

More than any of the other chapters, this one is rooted squarely in the Hawaiian belief in *'ohana.* To seek and yearn for belonging is a profoundly human need. In the world we currently inhabit, a staggering universe of opportunity and possibility is presented to us. Individuals in most advanced cultures can now increasingly enjoy endless variations on self-realization. But as these opportunities grow, we stretch the ties that bind us to the breaking point. If we lose sight of where we're from, what we're made of, and who our people are, we run the danger of "disappearing." *'Ohana* not only uses the connection and the community of the Now to undertake what the tribe needs and desires. It is a reminder that everything we do involves a relentless reconnection with our ancestors—the invocation of every brilliant creature that has led to us and the moment we are in. To call on the resilience and mettle of every creature that has gone before us and survived, repeatedly, again and again, down through the years, across millennia and among like-minded creatures—why would I not want to connect and commune with that? That's the power of *'ohana.* And in a world where "community" is traded as a euphemism for digital profiteering, a small daily reminder that it is rooted, first and foremost, in physical proximity and emotional understanding is a good thing to have.

A Simple Exercise in Owning It

For Laird, his whole life, his whole journey, has been toward belonging, whether he realized it at the time or not. His sense of connection, both to the unique creature that he is and the people and culture he grew up around, is irrepressible.

To begin this journey, Laird had to break away. He "transgressed" the boundaries of his island life and his own physicality and capability. He turned the very things that confined him into the things that defined him. He owned everything about himself. Grasped it. Poked it. Smashed it. Worked it. No stone left unturned; his unbridled curiosity turned on himself first and foremost. A truth seeker, starting with himself.

In this we find a salutary lesson. Whoever we are, whatever we've done, whatever we're made of, wherever we're from, whosoever we've been and whatever our failings, it's all us. Once we stop running from it all; once we turn and embrace it. No excuses. Look it in the eye. And own it. We have a foundation for everything we desire or dream to be.

To own it, we need to understand and be content with why we're here, what we're doing, how we're doing it, and why we're doing it. And that requires a perspective that reaches far beyond the individual's.

For example: Take the most laborious, mind-numbing task you might have to do. Think about what had to come before it to enable you to undertake it—the people involved prior to you, the materials, the small tasks, the journeys, the actions, the craft, the industry, the conversations, the interactions.

Cutting the grass is a good one. You and a lawn mower. An ordinary, everyday occurrence. But draw a line backward to the beginning and what do we find? We find the prospectors and miners and metalworkers and ore that make the raw steel and the machine's engine parts. We find the engineers modeling the blades. The testing over generations of which blade, which direction, which angle. Roller or no roller. Styles of cutting—circles versus horizontals. Seasonal differences. We find the engine builders, and the gasoline and electricity that drive the mower. We find the gardener's skills and expertise. We find the production operation, the assembly, the packing and shipping.

It takes all of these people and actions to bring us to the Now. So you cut the grass. Then, once you've cut it: How's it used? Games. Picnics. Eye candy. What outcomes? What consequences? And who will enjoy or use them? And how many times? Over how many years?

Now think of a person at every step of that journey. You may know the people. You may not. They may be long past or yet to be born. But imagine each of them with equal vividness, grinding out their task or undertaking their action. Every one of them, and you, is part of the particular evolution of that task. To be happy in that—to be happy in even the most banal motions of life—is to own who you are and the life you have. The killer app for contentedness.

SOUL

"Your soul is connected with your breath."

—LAIRD HAMILTON

THE world is accelerating. Technology has got us moving at fiber-optic speed, fracturing our identities across multiple platforms, devices, and networks, enabling us to do an amazing number of things at ever faster speeds, both individually and collectively.

But in the midst of that hectic and exhilarating life, we're forgetting to breathe.

Breathing does more than just keep us alive. It aligns us, balances us, and helps us to maintain and repair ourselves under duress. Now more than ever, we need to be aware of what the simplest act of breathing can do for us.

Ancient breathing techniques have evolved with us over

thousands of years as an offset to the extremity of the conditions in which our ancestors existed, and in which they sought to realize a greater self.

But science is starting to reveal to what degree breathing not only can enhance physical performance and general well-being, but also help us to manage pain thresholds and act as an intrinsic part of the intuitive mechanisms within us.

Breath sits at the crossroads of two dimensions in us that are at their best when working in an integrated, interrelated manner.

Here Laird explores the role of breath not only as the well of physical performance, recovery, and pain management, but also as the well of our mental and spiritual resilience and our ability to connect to ourselves and the world around us.

He explores how we draw on that well, in very particular terms, for very particular reasons.

And he demonstrates that, for those of us who choose to go there, a wealth of human riches awaits to be tapped with every breath we take.

> The average person takes approximately 20,000 breaths a day and more than 100 million breaths throughout a lifetime (Hendricks, 1995).
>
> — AMY HEATH, HEATHER MASHUGA, AND ANN ARENS,
> "EFFECTS OF A CONSCIOUS BREATHING INTERVENTION
> ON EMOTION AND ENERGY FLOW"

LAIRD

When you come into existence, when you come into life, the first thing you do is breathe. You come out of the womb, they slap your butt, and you breathe in. You take the first, and one of two of your most profound breaths—the other being the last one.

At the point of this first baby breath, we could debate about whether or not the spirit comes into you. But, as far as the ancients and most belief systems are concerned, the breath and the spirit are as one. They are connected.

But that's the spiritual side of things, that's the ethereal or the invisible or the unknown that maybe will never be known. We can debate the existence of the unknown endlessly. But right now the science, the data, isn't there.

But we instinctually feel it—the connection between breath and when life begins and when it ends—when death happens.

We have machines that cheat this now, but at an organism level—your breath stops and, as far as we in this life are concerned, your spirit or your conscious, sentient self is gone.

People stop breathing and their spirit leaves their body. Breath is the doorway both to life and to death. It's central at that moment of transcendence. Whether you believe that moment of transcendence is particular, and a whole load of atoms start to rearrange themselves into something else in the cosmos, or whether it's a spiritual or metaphysical journey—looking back and seeing the white light, that whole thing—the breath and the soul are connected. That's how powerful the relationship is.

In life we have a tendency to overlook the most obvious thing, which is that to survive, to exist, we have to breathe. Breathing is living. Breathing is attached to our conscious self. Being alive.

Without food, we can last for weeks; and without water we can last for days. But without breathing we can last for minutes—and so, in the priority of existence, breathing is really important.

When you're connected to the ocean you have a good relationship with the importance of breath, because it's attached to drowning as a result of not being able to breathe.

So if you're living and playing on the ocean—kitesurfing, diving, surfing, sailing, whatever—you have a pretty good relationship with breath; you have a pretty sharp awareness of the importance of breath. But in a very specific way. In this world, my world, it's linked directly to survival. Get this wrong; be ignorant; be arrogant—you're dead. You are straight to death.

For athletes, it's a different realization. It's your fuel. But in normal circumstances, in society, we are very unaware of breath and its importance.

And we mostly have no idea of what breath can do for us. We don't give it the credence, the respect, it deserves. We don't take the time to really understand its role within us, who we are and what we're capable of.

You have specific yoga breathing techniques, and free divers have techniques, and psychologists have techniques—all these different people have these different techniques for breathing that have all these different effects. But we kind of trip over them, right? We tend to come into them accidentally or randomly.

We don't do this as a matter of course. In ancient cultures and civilizations, this was normal. These techniques were everyday things. They were linked to survival.

We have specific disciplines of breath work that we do—that have these values that affect our physicality, that affect our emotional state. Every one of them is connected to our wellness, but most of us just sit there and we breathe. It never really occurs to us that this thing happening right under our nose could be like a turbo-booster for us; we never consider the amazing things it could allow us to do.

We breathe through our mouths. We don't even think about how important it is. And how little you have to do to make that a whole lot better.

As soon as you bring awareness into the breath, it changes your relationship with your breathing. As soon as you bring awareness into it, you create an importance around it—a focus. We know it's important, but we increasingly need to be reminded of that.

One of my theories is that the reason why we love to exercise is because it's forced breathing.

My theory is that our unconscious mind is putting our conscious mind up to some work—saying, *Hey, I need you to breathe, I know you're not disciplined enough to breathe without doing something, so let's start moving. Let's put some pressure on. Let's stress that system a little.*

If you run, you're going to breathe, and then that's going to give you what the body wants. You will get more oxygen in. You'll be pushing the CO_2 out—scraping out the CO_2—helping the machine run.

That's why the body rewards you for exercise.

The body's telling you: *The only way I know I can get what I need is to get you to do this through activity. But I know that to get you to ride your bike, go on a run, do something, I've got to get you hooked to it. I need you to love it. In fact, I kind of want you to get addicted to it. So I'm going to reward you; I'm going to give you a load of chemicals that make you feel good.*

That's evolution at work right there. There are a particular set of switches that need to be thrown to keep the organism at maximum performance. And if the organism has figured out across thousands if not millions of years that we need a reward for that, evolution is going to make that happen. Evolution comprehends the importance of breathing to the system—the volume, the amount—and acts accordingly, putting the systems in place to make sure it happens.

Now, if I do what the unconscious wants me to do, and I receive that bag of goodies, all those endorphins, now I'm aware of the feeling it gives me. Now I respect it. I don't only know, intellectually or academically, that its important. I *feel* it.

So now what am I going to do? Well, I want more rewards, right? I'm going to designate time. I'm going to do *pranayama* [breath work], or I'm going to do free diving, or I'm going to do holotropic breathing techniques, or I'm going to get a little monkish and do Tummo—or I'm going to try the "Iceman" Wim Hof's techniques.

And when you breathe deeper, the unconscious is going, *More of that please*, and suddenly, really quickly, you're moving yourself into a structure.

But you have to give this focus. You have to give it space. That's why specific isolation of the cardiovascular system, where you isolate the breath or breathing pattern, is good.

Whatever you might be doing—lying on the mat doing yoga; you might be doing some stretches in your front room, or something like that—but simply by becoming aware of the breath, you're isolating the whole cardiovascular system.

The most intense breathing can be done lying down anywhere.

You could do one of the most organism-stressing breath workouts lying on the floor in your own front room, or in the park, or on a gym mat.

The stillness allows adaptation and expansion. When you're static, you're not using so much energy to rebuild the muscles and clean up the damage of the breath exhaust from working out.

If you go running, you're using your cardiovascular system, but your cardiovascular system is just trying to keep up with the amount of work that your muscles are doing, so you have to feed the muscle—take out the bad stuff, put the good stuff back in, and so forth. So you're not getting to work on your capacity. You're simply stressing the system.

But if you're only working on increasing capacity, then you're going to become more efficient—you're going to be able to use the extra oxygen intake, and the improved absorption of it and all the strength of that—and you're going to get the benefits of the CO_2 reduction to develop and make that system more efficient.

And once the system's more efficient, you can implement it into stuff.

You can start implementing it into activity with this new increased efficiency and these new patterns—and a deeper relationship with it, right?

We start to affect the way the organism works. Improve it. Take it to a whole new level.

All of that can come from sitting in the room and just practicing breathing for an hour or two hours—or whatever time you can give it.

When we're doing breath work we really are working on

the "in and out"—how it feels to fully expand the lungs to create increased volume. And your lungs are pretty flexible things—they say the lung is flexible enough to stretch over a football field; but it's being held captive in our posture.

Everyday life and stress just make that captive situation worse. If our shoulders are like rock—if we're in fight-or-flight mode—if we're super tight—and our abs are ripped—we have no volume. There's no room, so we need to learn to create volume, especially in those moments when we're under duress. We need to learn to create volume by expanding and then topping up.

By sipping more air in, expanding and pushing and driving the breath into the groin, you can create expansion which is going to result in your efficiency increasing.

This technique will get you to full oxygenation—full saturation. And you're going to feel it—in your lips, in your ears, all the extremities. But you'll also realize that suddenly, on the breath out, everything works harder—and you can do more push-ups, more routines, more reps.

If you haven't improved that efficiency, you do an activity and the necessity for oxygen—and ultimately the necessity to get rid of the CO_2—demands that the breath rate increases. Instead of being ahead of the game and learning how to increase volume of oxygen and increase CO_2 before the necessity arises, you can never catch up.

But you can get in front and stay ahead of the need through that deeper relationship with the breath—through creating conscious breathing. That's evolution right there.

But the first step is for us all to realize that most of the time we're just under-oxygenated—we're oxygen-deprived.

I think a lot of the problem with the breathing gurus—

trendy techniques and yoga and retreats and stuff—is that it looks like you've got to be on another planet to get it or do it. It looks exclusive. It just doesn't seem relevant to the lives most people lead.

Pictures of people doing stretches and *pranayama* on a mat under palm trees at sunset on a tropical island or on top of a mountain—like, really? If I have to jump a commuter train packed with grumpy assholes every day—or sit in an office in the middle of a business park—how does that work? Where's my palm tree? That's just going to piss me off, right?

But breath awareness can be done anywhere, anytime.

For example, you know that thing when you've had your headphones on and suddenly the song's finished or it's not jumped to the next track—what do you hear? Your breathing—right up in your ears. Really loud. There's your moment right there. On a train, a bus, anywhere.

In that moment. Get aware.

Just listen to your breath, listen to your breathing, the rhythm of it, and then modulate it. Play with it. Take it a little deeper. Use your diaphragm. Slow it. Speed it up. Take bigger gaps between breaths. That's conscious breathing. You can do that anywhere. When you start listening, you'll start improving.

The saying is: "Your breath has a voice; make it speak." And when it does: listen. We need to remember that the relationship between us and our bodies is two-way, right? When it speaks, we need to listen. And we need to respond to it. And conscious breathing is the door to that.

I can't tell you how many times we do breath work and these people are breathing, big openmouthed breathing, and I say, "Do me a favor now; please breathe—because if you're running in a race and you're breathing like that, you're not going to be running very fast."

It's always back to the same place. It's back to conscious awareness and your relationship with your breath. Hear your breath—feel your breath—right?

Once you're feeling your breath, once you've got the measure of it, you can stick with that level—or you can go further. You can go into nose breathing—Oxygen Advantage stuff. Or using a combination of nose and mouth breathing to oxygenate and scrub CO_2.

Athletes are healthier because they get all the benefits of the breathing process—though you would be surprised: we are not all as healthy as we could be, because we don't all have a good relationship with our breath.

There's another thing that puts the public off. They look at all these athletes and think, *I just can't do what they do. I can't develop like that.* Well, if we're talking breathing you may be surprised. You might already be ahead of them.

It's pretty common in many athletes to have a bad relationship with breathing. There is some ridiculous percentage of athletes who are below the average of the public when it comes to their cardiovascular efficiency.

And you'll find it's the same thing. It doesn't matter if we're an athlete or not. If you're not conscious, if you're not nose breathing, you're running half-empty.

I can take a group of athletes and watch them breathe and I'm like, "Buddy, you guys are Olympic sprinters; you're football players; you're professionals—I mean, this is what you do . . . so please, breathe!"

They don't know how to breathe! And they don't know how to breathe because they've never been taught how to breathe. They've never connected with their breath. But I get it. If you don't understand the importance of it, why would you know it?

For me, stuff has to be relevant. I can't do the hypothetical or theory stuff. I can become really aware, really conscious of something, as long as I understand its value, right? If it's relevant and important, I am doing it. Because it's got a clear function in my life.

Maybe that's a Hawaiian thing. Conscious, mindful action. Everything is applied to a task. Hawaiian spirituality is always applied to tasks that help the community.

There is no disconnect. I'm reaching into the most spiritual sources of myself, but only for a reason—to do something practical—something meaningful—make a boat, catch a fish, surf a reef.

[According to the ancient Hawaiians, human beings have three souls]:

Lower Soul: is located close to solar plexus—the "mind that never sleeps"—but permeates the entire body.

Middle Soul: "the mind that talks" is the conscious, walking, thinking mind that reasons, uses logic and makes decisions. It resides in the head.

Upper Soul: is the personal connection to the higher source. The High self—is the source of the insights, inspiration and absolute love. It is generally felt to be above the body.

—CHARLOTTE BERNEY,

FUNDAMENTALS OF HAWAIIAN MYSTICISM

If breathing helps me do something a whole lot better and I've got a real applicable reason to be doing it, I'm in. I'll do the breathing thing. And build myself up. And do stuff better. And it's also an "I don't want to drown" thing, for sure.

So, before I was exposed to any type of breath work, I used to mimic some of the things that I experienced when I was on the water.

Before I became formally aware of hypoxic training and the Oxygen Advantage, I was already doing that stuff— thirty years ago.

I was doing breath-holding between bouts of strenuous exercise. I'd run the beach and then I'd breathe and then I'd hold my breath and breathe and hold my breath to mimic what I was going to do; what I was going to experience in my surfing.

I was mimicking my experiences and my understanding of the environment in which I wanted to exist. Mimicking the way that if I get hit by a wave, the water takes you, pushes you down, takes you away from the air, keeps you there, rolls you.

Mimicking environment is powerful. If you look at the world and respond to it in those terms, knowledge is really everywhere. Mimicking and practicing what the environment or the circumstance might present to us, how it might stress us, is how we learn.

That's us being respectful of the fact that evolution's smarter than us. Evolution has the advantage, as it has no time limit and no budget—endless time—no restraints—no opinions and no motive—except to be efficient.

Mimicking those kinds of breath stresses is really a form of mimicking evolution.

So the meditative state around breathing—an awareness, a consciousness—is good. Anyone that's doing any kind of breath work at all, they'll always bring it back to meditation—because of the state that it puts you in.

Learning how to be CO_2 tolerant and then making the lungs more efficient—becoming more efficient at breathing, and becoming more connected to your breath? There's no one that doesn't benefit from that.

That's not just about not dying. That's about more living. Being more alive.

It's also about very specific stuff, like pain management. Breathing techniques can be used to manage pain thresholds and acute pain situations.

Breathing can be used as a recovery technique. It's powerful in more ways than I think many people realize. "It's just breathing, right? What's the big deal?"

But the role of breathing, not as just a source of energy but as healer—as a way of controlling pain and also managing fear through the autonomic system—is central.

But it isn't just how we breathe and our conscious awareness of it that directly affects the performance of our breathing.

Everything is connected. And our diet has a whole lot to do with how well the organism's breathing functions work, both in terms of nutrition and in terms of the effects of food and eating on the system generally.

One of the things we notice right now whenever we do breath work—you want an empty stomach. You don't want to eat anything—you don't want to do workouts on a full stomach. That's not the kind of energy you need to load up on before a workout. You need to load up on the right kind of breathing. Let's remember what oxygen is—oxygen is energy. Period. It's the only energy we need, certainly before a workout. It's the number one energy in our system.

Breath is part of the holistic process of the organism. Every single process in the body uses oxygen or is served by oxygen in some way, either directly or indirectly. Every single process is connected to oxygen. So in the priority of what's important, it's at the top. You can live a long time breathing; you don't live a very long time without it.

Heart is ruler—oxygen doesn't go anywhere without the heart. But breath is what keeps everything on. It's what keeps the "light" on. That's the link to our conscious self.

But it's worth remembering that, as we said with the body, it's always worth stressing the organism—because we really have only just begun to tap what's within us. Evolution has put so much in the tank that we are still totally unaware of. Capabilities, competencies that are currently beyond our imagination.

There's an Indian guy who does this particular breath technique. I can't remember whether it's an inhale or an exhale. He does it on a microphone. This single breath goes on for what seems like five minutes, and it makes you wonder—how's a guy breathing for that amount of time? There are amazing things that happen at the edges of our ability as an organism.

Only on the fringes of an ecosystem, those outer rings, do evolution and adaptation occur at a furious pace; the inner center of the system is where the entrenched, non-adapting species die off, doomed to failure by maintaining the status quo.

—YVON CHOUINARD, *LET MY PEOPLE GO SURFING*

You become aware that on the outer edges of us there's a transcendent point, and breath is involved in that. Hawaiians believe that if you breathe in the exhale of a dolphin, that's like superpowerful. This exchange is somehow a super-exchange of life force—of energy.

Now, some people may find all of the outer edges of breath mythology and mysticism a little hard to take. But who knows. Perhaps, like in so many other things, if your instinct tells you it's right, the math, the data, or the science of it may just pop up one day to prove it.

In islander mysticism, to all of the Polynesian people, breath is everything.

When the Maoris meet and they put their noses together. When they rub noses and breathe out, they are exchanging *ha*.

Indirectly I know the value of breath to the islanders. Not always for great reasons, of course. I grew up a *ha'ole*, remember—what the Hawaiians call white men. *Ha'ole*: "without the breath of life."

Ha is the sacred breath of life within us all, or the spirit of the Creator that breathes life into all living beings, and breathing practice is called *ha huna*.

In Hawaii, there are native kahuna doctors that use the life energy concept of mana in their healing practices. By breathing deeply and visualizing mana, there is a positive effect on well-being, physical strength, senses, and the mind.

— AMY HEATH, HEATHER MASHUGA, AND ANN ARENS,
"EFFECTS OF A CONSCIOUS BREATHING INTERVENTION
ON EMOTION AND ENERGY FLOW"

In one of these festivals we would do this chant that was very *haka*-ish. Now I know the *haka* is a breath drill. Yes, it's a warrior intimidation—but it's a preparation for battle. A preparation for one of the most stressful physical undertakings someone will ever have to go through. The act of fighting for one's life.

The inhale/exhale—the nature of how they stress it through the *haka*—that's CO_2 scrubbing, and driving greater oxygenation to the system. That's maximum physical preparation through breath.

These are old practices rooted in the very basic biological and physiological truths of us as organisms, and in relation to our survival.

Breath as power. In martial arts you have *kiai*—and the importance of that in channeling energy and focusing action.

When the warrior is using breath, the *sound* of that breath—the volume of the breath exhale—is a way of demonstrating lung volume; capacity. The bigger the capacity, the greater their power. That's the roar of the warrior. The proof of their physical potential.

If I look back, I probably can see times when, other than the ocean being the ultimate kind of recognizer of the importance of oxygen—I can see times where all that Polynesian mysticism—all the dance; all the chants—have shaped me in some way. They are all breath.

One big circle, I guess. Breathing in terms of performance and surfing, but what it's done is it's brought me in a great big circle back to that Hawaiian culture.

So breath sits between the scientific and the spiritual—with the science continuing to confirm what we intuitively knew or spiritually believed.

But that's storytelling—and that's the problem with storytelling sometimes. The way in which a belief or a theory is presented can make us block it out—make us think, *Hey, that's not for me.*

It feels too metaphysical to some folks. Or, for some, it all gets a little cultish.

I'm not into the cultish. I don't do the guru thing. I see the guys and I watch the way they set themselves up—I suppose they exist because people want to have somebody lead them like that. It's not for me. It's not about the responsibility of doing that. It's more about the honesty of it.

It's not about leaders or gurus. It's about embarking on the journey together. It's a moment of *'ohana*—setting out together. To discover something together.

It's about sharing. "Let me share with you the things that I've experienced—things that for example I have discovered or know about breathing—and you can try them." There's just different ways of presentation which I think make a big difference.

I just want people to enjoy unlocking that stuff inside them. Throwing the switches and hopefully feeling a little of what I feel.

I think there's too much "head" stuff going on sometimes. I think we need a little *un*-mindfulness. This is as much about the unknown as it is about the known.

Part of the overthinking of it all is that I think we are a little lazy. "If I do a little mindfulness, live the hashtag, then I've done it"—kind of a smart, efficient way of missing out on all the real hard work.

We are looking for the path of least resistance—just give me the pill, let me just practice mindfulness. For me, if somebody goes, "Oh, you know I meditate," I would say, "That's great, but how about you just breathe?"

If the least you do is that, then you can say you meditated too. Because to meditate on something is to be conscious of it. "Meditation" has been hijacked as a word to be about some kind of monkish existence. It's not. It's just about being aware.

And it has very little to do with some kind of idea of comfy relaxation that people have.

Discomfort has to be a part of it.

I met these Buddhist monks that were staying at a friend's house, and we were sitting there in the lotus—or my version of the lotus, which is like a half-lotus.

We're there in the position for some time, and at the point when we were finished I said to the guy that was sitting next to me, "How long does it take before you get used to it? When does it become, you know, comfortable?"

He looked at me and said, "Well, it never becomes comfortable—it's meant to be uncomfortable—that's what keeps you present and aware."

So, there are people thinking these guys are just sitting there, somehow achieving this relaxed position through super-unstressful breathing, as perceived by the way their posture is—that they're in this zone—but there's no relaxation. That's the point. That's where the intensity comes from.

So breath is just kind of incredible. It is one of the things that lights up the brilliant creature that we are—and in so many ways. Biological, physiological, neuropathological, emotional, spiritual.

We can even use this stuff like self-powered triage. Guys like Wim Hof have shown that you can transcend the normal confines of breathing to such a degree that you can even use breathing to scrape your system to get rid of something like a bacterial infection or a virus.

All of this is simply more proof to me that between the scientific and the spiritual there are multiple things happening on multiple levels. I always say that there's a physical manifestation of every emotional sensation—and there's always an emotional manifestation of every physical sensation.

It's never really any one thing—everything is connected.

BAREFOOT BUSINESS

Soul, curiosity, and living, breathing innovation

Curiosity and innovation are the breath of life to any entrepreneur or business leader trying to create something meaningful and lasting.

Curiosity is the unconscious breath—the foundation and the base material of any thriving business.

A culture of relentless questioning—*Why? What? When? Where? Who? How?*—turning over every rock and stone in pursuit of something better—is what drives businesses forward—even in those business-as-usual moments.

And innovation is the conscious breathing that shapes performance, stamina, and strength.

Both are essential to a balanced company firing on all cylinders.

But they demand awareness—and the ability to tap into them at will. They need to be exercised, nurtured, and improved, in every kind of business.

And everything affects them. Purpose, culture, emotional disposition, company structure, and ultimately vision.

Here, Laird and Gabby explore how their relentless curiosity and taste for innovation are the living, breathing center of all of their businesses. We explore how Laird applies the *'ohana* principle toward creating a team of collaborators around one pure goal. And how both Gabby's intimate understanding of Laird and her natural nose for the commercial help to keep their businesses authentic and true.

LAIRD

I think I'm naturally curious, and I try to retain that as best I can. To continue to be curious. I think that's one of the fountains of youth; to retain your youthful enthusiasm ultimately means to retain your curiosity, because that's where you learn.

Why do kids learn so quickly? Because they're curious about everything; they're interested in everything. So, for me, I feel that's a big part of who I am naturally as a person. I cultivate that curiosity because I'm always looking for new ways to learn, or new information to open me up. And what you notice is, the more open you are, the more consistently stuff comes to you.

So I don't measure myself or my businesses by anyone. But I do stay open and look to learn from people.

Businesses like GoPro inspire me. GoPro's a pretty cool business because they've been the only one in the category. The original concept is so simple: *How do I make a camera so I can surf with it?*

It's always interesting to see a business that creates a category, I kind of like that. These businesses don't always survive, but in a way that's cool—because they inspire more businesses like them. The real success of these kinds of businesses isn't distribution; it isn't because they had financial backing; it isn't manufacturing; it's conceptual. They've carved a new space.

When you look at companies like Yamaha and Honda— those are some badass businesses, because they're always on the cutting edge. But at scale. They pretty much make the best stuff in the world in their category. Nobody in those categories can compete with them. In motor technology, who can really compete with Yamaha except Honda, and who can compete with Honda except Yamaha?

Maybe I'm biased. Maybe I really like them because they have a bunch of stuff I like to use—that might be swaying my interest. But they do inspiring stuff—they're constantly innovating—innovating, innovating, innovating. I like that aspect too. In innovation they are constantly sparring with their own and each other's potential.

How can we make this better? How can we continue to improve?

And in GoPro's world, they went into a space where there was a lot of shit out there already, by the way. It's not like there weren't cameras—there's a lot of cameras out there.

Also, where you pitch this stuff pricewise is critical. I think it's the art of it. How you price innovation to allow for maximum take-up without crashing its value. That's about creating access. Affordability.

GoPro probably could have done more expensive items—they could be a lot more expensive than they are. But they're making it so people can actually get their products and get out there and use them.

But innovation, keeping creative, is also tied into community. It ties into who you hang out with—what they are doing—what are they exposing you to—what are they talking to you about—it's all part of that. I have friends that are constantly interested in new stuff, seeking cool stuff out, and they're always sending me stuff. Gabby's always in stuff. Everybody that I'm around kind of has a similar mentality—so they're all looking.

If you're curious, then you're probably going to relate to

other curious people, and then you're going to be around curious people—birds of a feather.

It's not just coming up with new stuff. It's problem solving, because your curious nature helps resolve stuff, get through challenges; that's what it does.

If you are open to being surrounded by that, being fed by it—I think knowledge is abundant and available everywhere you look.

I think I could sit in this boat right here and I could learn about everything in the universe, if I was just open and interested and connected to the right people.

But I don't use other people as a reference for where I'm at. I never do that; I never have. I think that's a mistake.

It doesn't mean I can't appreciate somebody else's performance—or, in a business, appreciate somebody else's success. I just think that, ultimately, if I believe myself to be so different, or even if it's something that's similar—it's me doing it.

You can't expect to be the only one that has a good idea. With all the people in the world, the idea that someone somewhere wouldn't have similar ideas simultaneously? I think that's unrealistic—it's going to happen.

But *you* are the difference. Similar becomes different when an individual takes it and makes it.

I can see how using someone as a reference or benchmark might boost you a little bit—if somebody's having a success in your area, you check them out—or you try something someone else is doing and you think, *That's interesting, that's cool*—but you have to make it your own.

Your unique twist will always be unique—it will always be something special.

I think that innovation process comes from my own natural evolution—my desire to continue to evolve—to look for something new, to make and keep something interesting.

What fuels that? I think it comes from my nature—my tendency to get kind of bored quickly and not just accepting the monotony of the status quo, the continual monotony of the single thing, but just actually trying to make it interesting and new and exciting and different.

I would like to go into other areas. I have other ideas in other areas. But I can't just do blue-sky stuff. I think for me it needs to be a mix of the conceptual and the applicable—they both need to be at work.

For me, innovation has to be applicable. I am a doer. So I have a simple perspective: *What's your innovation? What's the application?* If it's just blue sky, well that's just a postcard, right? I just happen to innovate things I want to apply. I think a real part of true innovation has to do with your ability to understand, right? Your ability to understand its application.

I've been involved in some stuff where people go, "I thought of that years ago." But I go, "Well yeah, but if you did then you didn't fully understand what it meant; that's why you didn't evolve it further like we did."

I do think there is a skill at innovating, and that once you do it—the more you do it—the better you get at it—the better you can cultivate that, and so you can start to implement it in different areas.

Once you have kind of a formula, you could probably go to a business and look at it and go, "Hey, you should try this, try that" kind of thing—because I think there is a certain formula aspect to innovation that can be implemented in a variety of backdrops—once you've done it a few times. Like the formula for success we were talking about. You can start to apply it in other fields, other areas.

It seems like, right now, real innovation comes from hybrids—where you combine a couple different things together. I think we've had so many innovations over history that a lot of them are taken up—but if we combine them, then they become a new one.

I use the simple ones that I've been involved with as an example. If you take paddling and you take surfing—put them together and you have stand-up paddle surfing.

As the saying goes: "There's nothing new; it's just a new application of an old idea."

And those ideas have to keep flowing, right? There's all kinds of stuff that you're always thinking about—you'll have a hundred ideas and two that work. There's always something to inspire you; usually a problem to be solved.

So many innovations are based on some kind of problem solving. That's really the purest basis of innovation—to problem solve—how do we fix something that we're having a problem with, and what's the most efficient way to do that?

Innovation is just the evolutionary principle commercialized.

I've had one idea on my brain for a while, inspired by the work I'm doing on the new house, where I'm clearing a lot of the plot. I had this idea for cleaning away undergrowth using high-pressure, high-temperature water, but it ended up that people are already doing it—people already had a product based on it.

But I still want to work on the idea—on how you can kill heavy-duty weeds and heavy growth with hot water, removing any kind of chemical or toxin from the process and just using extreme temperature.

And this needs to be powerful. There are some tough plants on this island—species of plants that are wreaking havoc. So I've got a good test bed for what the application needs to deliver.

So my point here is that idea generation is joined to my feeling about the applicable nature of innovation.

It's also back to the authenticity point. This idea is fixed in a real need for me directly; a need that has revealed a bigger, more commercially applicable one. My innovation comes from my mindful action and an immediate functional need.

But the key here isn't just inspiration: it's work rate. Application is not just about the idea's role in the world. It's about your commitment *to* the idea. This stuff takes a lot of tending. A lot of nurture.

With the foil boards, we've been doing R&D for as long as we've been doing them. Small. Incremental. Shape. Test. Measure. Evolve.

We'd make little changes, get a new piece. Change a line. Try different compounds. We've been chipping away at that thing, getting better, and getting better stuff. Improving the shape—improving the material—it doesn't end.

But our foil board innovation process doesn't begin and end with the guys at Oracle [the America's Cup ORACLE TEAM USA—collaborators in Laird's foil innovation]. That's the most systemized, scale-innovation partnership we have. But that's not all of it.

When you are innovating, you need to be open to everything—all scales and natures of partnership.

I've always done this. Pulled teams together around things I'm trying to do something different with—around innovation. In that way, in reality, I am using a collaboration model where you draw the best people around a shared goal.

So I'm also collaborating with other much smaller concerns and individuals. I've got three different people that I'm working with. They build stuff; they're trying products, they send them to me; I'm giving them feedback—and then they improve.

Between Oracle and these guys, I'm using an ecosystem of innovation partners to do what I want to do. Using multiple fronts to keep the evolution moving.

GABBY

Laird is relentless. He's just this curious kid. Like I said, Dennis the Menace and a scientist all rolled up in one. But he's very true to his own path. We're the same on that.

Comparing yourself or holding yourself up to competitors all the time—it's a distraction.

One time, me and Laird were in Newport Beach. It was like 1996 or 1997—I was doing a volleyball tournament down there and Laird, well, he was riding some really big waves at the time; I mean, they were making themselves available. So he's not really needing to prove anything to anyone. But Newport Beach is a very big surfing community with a very big surfing culture. There's a very particular thing going on there—the look, the wear, the talk. It's like heavy-duty. It's a *thing*, right?

So there we were, having breakfast. And Laird has shorts on; probably too short for that time—he's in his old T-shirt—and his hair's like, well, everywhere. So he's not falling into line with the Newport thing, right? And

I remember thinking to myself, *He doesn't have time to understand, know, or study what the style of a surfer is or should be—because he's too busy* doing *it and* being *it.*

And I think that's true of most things. If you're spending so much time looking side to side, you can't get on your path. But equally, if somebody out there is doing some really good work—even though it's close to the work you're doing—you better fucking love it, because then you're liberated to celebrate all of it—not just your own stuff.

Relentless self-checking and comparison with your competition just dampers you in a way. It blocks your mind; it blocks flow; it blocks your ideas; and I think it makes you limited.

But if you're like, "*Yo!* Awesome. Nice work," that celebration of someone else's achievements frees you.

Laird has it easily, it's just innate in him. Instead of feeling threatened, his response is, "I'm going to look and I'm going to celebrate everything that's great about that and what they're doing."

That mindset really helps when you're an entrepreneur, because that also makes you more collaborative. It's not threatening when people within your group shine or do something badass.

Listen

It's all getting a little hectic out there. We're forgetting to breathe. The result is that many of us end up tired, wired, and oxygen-deprived. We spend an enormous amount of our time fighting through the noise of our lives. And it's getting noisier, fueled by the multiple voices we broker into the world through social media and our networks of engagement. Our work self, our play self, our e-mail self, our Twitter self, our Facebook self, our Instagram self. Add to these the teeming expanding conversations each one of these selves engages in, and the volume just increases exponentially. There are good aspects to this way of life. But equally there are downsides. It's getting harder to hear our body's "voice" amid the white noise.

Laird is a great proponent of conscious breathing. Breathing that we *listen to* and can focus on—the rhythm of it, the depth and duration of it—is the most powerful form of breathing that we can master. With each breath, we draw ourselves deeper into the middle of ourselves, and further away from the cacophonous noise that surrounds us. The more we fill our chests and empty our minds, the closer we come to transcending our ordinary self.

Transcendence can seem like a luxury to anyone who struggles with bills at the end of every month. But transcendence is not the sole preserve of people up a mountain on some retreat from the world. Each one of us carries the tools of transcendence within us.

Laird views breathing as one of the great tools of the physical and the spiritual self. A tool by which we can expand lung capacity and oxygenation levels to enhance and improve stamina and performance; but also a tool of introspection—a tool that we can use to turn inward and truly listen to our bodies.

Laird is the greatest advocate of such listening. He believes that to embrace the brilliant creature that we are, we need to learn to listen to our bodies relentlessly, and to trust what we are hearing. And we need to respond to it. Through listening we can respond meaningfully to the body's ever-changing state, and interact with its myriad faculties. Consciousness is simply the interface between us and the staggeringly complex set of systems and processes within us. For Laird, breathing is the most obvious and visible manifestation of that—a healthy dialogue between us and the brilliant creature that we are. Laird believes that in the reciprocal nature of this interaction between our inner and outer selves lies a key to our ability to ride the turbulence of life. If we are not *listening*, we are not being whole. So here the two values we are building on are **trust** and **reciprocity**. With our breath as the tie that binds them.

TRUST

Laird is a trusting man. It is a point of clarity for him—it is foundational. For Laird, trust is not just a social condition established solely to guide the integrity and actions of people and institutions. His concept of trust is founded in something far more ancient—faith in the organism we are. For Laird, his starting point for trust lies in what he believes the human organism can do; what it is capable of. The genetic wisdom invested in us is something that Laird has every faith in. His intuition is something he trusts to tell him things science does not yet know about the natural world and the unseen laws that guide how he, as a living organism, needs to exist within it. He trusts in *unknown unknowns*—regardless of their currently being, and possibly always staying, beyond our comprehension. He trusts in the logic, order, and permanence of things—of measurable cause and effect—as much as he trusts in the chaos, disorder, and impermanence of things—the ability of life, nature, people, and circumstances to throw things at us seemingly from nowhere. And he trusts in the path that exists between the two as our natural and most honest state.

In trusting these things, Laird is freed to trust that something as simple as conscious breathing can take him from the ordered, measured act of merely decompressing from training—or being a ramp to meditation—all the way through to transcendent states of being and a wealth of unimagined capability.

Without a simple, foundational trust in the organism, we stop listening; and we stop learning. And when we stop learning, we stop growing.

RECIPROCITY

The greatest reciprocity is that which exists between our conscious and unconscious selves. Our ability to listen to the many "voices" that our organism uses to communicate with our conscious self is critical to well-being. But this has to be a two-way street. We must maintain a reciprocal nature in these conversations with self. As we all know, if a friend keeps giving us advice and we continue to ignore it, they will eventually stop giving it.

We are a responsive creature. The organism has survived and thrived for this long because it is responsive to environment and circumstance. The systems of knowing housed in our genetic makeup have been formed through relentless testing and retesting, where the response to any situation or threat is critical to forming the best position on how best to deal with it when it next arises. The organism has coded this learning into every corner of our being. When the organism speaks to us, it deserves to be listened to. Moreover, it deserves to be respected and responded to. The exchange between us and the inner workings of the organism we are is vital to how we live a full and meaningful life.

'Ohana

Within *'ohana* there is a simple adherence by every individual to the nature of *ha*, or "the breath of life." This is the precious and most valuable gift that we have to give to the world. Communities are rooted in each individual's ability to use their *ha*, not just for themselves but as one part of the whole and for the mutual benefit of all. How we broker our life force in the world, starting with those closest to us and most reliant on us, is critical to building the most resilient social fabric. We must be able to rely on those next to us to think and do the same, willingly and reflexively. And they should be able to rely on our willingness to respond in kind.

'Ohana could not exist without trust and reciprocity as keystones. I can only engage in mutually beneficial exchanges of care and shared pursuit if I: (a) trust in the integrity of the people around me to act collectively in any given situation, and (b) understand that the exchange will be fair and balanced and active on both sides in the *'ohana* group, especially if it is under duress or threat. In a survival situation, I don't want to be navigating the basic tenets of *Do I trust the person next to me?* and *Will they always return everything I do for them in kind?* If there are multiple issues with either of those, the system will break down.

So, to bring the spirit of *'ohana* to life, we need to listen for trust and reciprocity, both within ourselves and in those closest to us.

A Simple Exercise in Listening

Listening to ourselves is critical to well-being. But it must be able to transcend the passive—it must be able to enter an active phase. To be able to perform at a higher level, consumed by the physical and mental aspects of the task, while still listening not only to your breathing but to everything your body is telling you "in the flow," is the difference between good and great. Action must not be an excuse for "deafness."

Listening must be active. A command to the self. And it should be elevating at the very least, and transcendent at its very best. Hence the mantra "listen up." Lift up your eyes from the task. Lift up your ears from the noise. And listen to yourself.

Trust what your body tells you. And reciprocate in kind. Your conscious self and the organism for which it interprets are a team. And that means teamwork.

Earlier, Laird pointed to headphones as a killer app for listening amid the scrum of everyday life and commuting hell. Headphones, especially the noise-canceling kind, elevate the sound of our breathing to a soundscape. So let's use them as a simple tool to "listen up." Make your own breathing the playlist for a day. Keep your headphones in, but keep the music and the podcasts on pause. Listen to nothing other than your own breathing. Listen to it as you climb stairs, walk the corridors, sit on the train. Listen to how your breathing sounds. Focus on it. Once you have the rhythm of listening, raise the game—start to open out to the feelings that you feel when you move. Hear how your breathing changes, and feel how your body responds. Feel the interrelated nature of body and breath as you move. With just ten minutes immersed in the soundscape of yourself each day, listening will become second nature. (And, for some, quite addictive.)

Everything Is Connected

We were in the Aha moment
We *were* the Aha moment.
And then we got knowledge;
And we slowly moved further
and further away from things.

—LAIRD HAMILTON

THE universe we're in is expanding. And we are expanding within it.

Technologies are the slingshot of our humanity. Brilliant technologies, relentlessly applied to greater and greater degree, have allowed us to match our biological evolution with a cultural evolution that has rocketed us to the top of the food chain.

We're in exciting times.

As the convergence of humanity and technology intensifies, we find ourselves coming to the edge of our previous existence as creatures. We are at a tipping point.

Some see a new dawn and a greater human brilliance still—a transcendent moment where man and machine converge into immortal protean Oneness.

Some see an arrogance allowing the development of a dark age for humanity, in which we will be lost in subservience to machines, ultimately leading to the obsolescence of our species as we know it.

But in finding a balance between what is known and un-known to us—in the space where the intuitive, instinctive nature of our old spiritual selves and the computational and accelerated capability of our current selves collide—we could perhaps find our greatest trajectory.

In this chapter, Laird explores the truly connected nature of the brilliant creature we are, the lives we lead, and the excep-tional nature of the connection between us and the world that surrounds us, both natural and social.

And he explores a little of his own hyper-connectedness, and the threads that bind him to his past, present, and future.

LAIRD

Everything is connected—your heart to your mind, to your sight, to your breath, to your skin, to your DNA, to your family, to your friends, to the environment, to your experi-ences, to your feelings, to your food, to pleasure, to pain, to the moment, to your memory, to your dreams, to com-munity, to culture, to energy, to matter, to vibrations, to the cosmos, to the beginning of time and to the end of it. Every-thing is just one relentless cycle of life and death and rebirth.

There's truth. There's honesty. For us as individuals. For humanity. For us as a species. But we seem to be losing our grip on that. So anything we can do that reasserts that truth is a good thing.

Every single thing affects you. If you think about your

system and what's in it, and what it needs and what it contains, what it manages and what it uses, we're a pretty joined-up creature.

Within us we have water—we have power—we have magnetic fields—we have genetic switches—we have unconscious and conscious physiological systems. We have neuropathological traits: we've got a whole lot of stuff wired up together. And that's before we even get to how we connect with everything and everybody around us.

This connectivity plays out in the smallest things. I was talking with a guy and he said, "I wanna get more flexible." So I'm like, "Well, are you hydrated? 'Cuz if you're not hydrated, don't even talk to me about being flexible. You're not even in a position to become flexible if you're not properly hydrated."

There was a time when we understood this. We understood how important the connection between everything is—but now it comes like a surprise. If someone is talking about flexibility, the last thing in your head is hydration—you wouldn't give that a second thought.

That's the kind of thoroughness you have to be aware of in the relationship that you have with all of the things that affect everything. You need to switch back to scrutinizing all of these things continuously. We used to. But as we got knowledge we lost the older connections.

Now we're like, "I'm not hydrated—I'm not sleeping well," or "My vision isn't sharp," and then we wonder why our hand-eye accuracy is not very good, or our balance is being affected.

Once we have reminded ourselves of how connected everything is, we change our response.

We start to take more interest. We realize that some

parts of the organism are weak or slack—or simply asleep. Suddenly we're testing the edges. Stressing stuff. Suddenly we're in continuous attendance to the organism. Eyesight, hydration, sleep, food, temperature, hearing, sensitivity, touch, feet! Everything affects the others. We just need to improve our awareness of that. Like breathing and what it impacts.

My vision is really important to me. That's why I have to be super attentive to my sight. So I use an app to do eye drills—exercises that train my eyes. That's why it's also good to go out into the dark. And when it's real bright. It stresses your visual faculty. But I also need to be aware of other stuff connected to my vision. Diet. Stress. Environment. And each of them needs to be viewed with the others in mind.

If your vision's compromised, if your hydration's compromised, if your nutrition's compromised, if your sleep's compromised—these are all interrelated to the effectiveness of the whole system.

And that means both sides, right? We're done with this academic division between the rational and the emotional. Between the scientific and intuitive. We know enough—about the autonomic system and the electromagnetic nature of our hearts and the synchronization between heart and brain—to not do that anymore. Call it holistic. Call it what you want. It's connectivity.

Everything affects everything. If you're having doubt; if you're having some mental issues—stressful working life, unhappiness—that's going to affect the system. Directly or indirectly.

Accepting that this is just the way of things—and that all of these things serve each other—means that you'll be more likely to figure out a way of managing things when bad or negative things happen, and in such a way as to help the system and keep balance.

Because the simple fact is, you're going to have negative thoughts. Unless you're Superman or Wonder Woman, and even then . . . you're going to have things that are negatively affecting you. You can't dodge that stuff. That's life. That's friction.

But it's how you respond to it that will make the difference. The negativity and the impact of that stuff lies in the way you react, not in the negative nature of the thought or the situation.

"Things don't freak him out—like, how he is when it's really giant out there is how he is when it's pretty difficult, even for himself emotionally.

"I don't think he tries to run from a really tough feeling or stuff it or hide it. He moves through it and to it. He doesn't try to justify it or move away from it—paint it a different color. He never runs away from his feelings—he openly weeps. He feels the suffering and he continues to move to it—because I think he feels that if he keeps just standing and being there, he can really look at it—and then be able to move on. I think if you never really look at it, whatever 'it' is—and your reaction to the 'it'—your feelings, your heartache—then it's just something that you pack inside. And Laird doesn't do that. He doesn't have so much stuff packed in there.

"He really feels it—he feels it all, and he doesn't have to wait years and years to feel it."

—GABBY REECE

You're either fighting yourself—getting hit by life, again and again—or you're riding this stuff.

You're either thinking, *I can't believe I'm having those thoughts*, and that will create a whole heap of conflicted and additional pressure—or, alternatively, you respond, *Oh yeah, that's normal—it's not great but it's normal, shit happens—I'll just push right by that or through it.*

The visible and the invisible are affecting your balance—your organism. Where your house is, who your neighbors are, where the wind's blowing. Are you waking up before the sun or are you waking up with the sun? What time are you going to bed? You can get ten hours of sleep a day, but if you go to bed at one o'clock in the morning after binging box sets or playing some computer game, soaking up all that screen glow—and if you're sleeping till noon—well, that's not good sleep. That's not properly restful. Which puts you on the back foot.

Rest is like hydration. You are either rested or you're not. And if you're not, that is going to affect all manner of other functions—physical, mental, and emotional.

But our connectivity reaches far, far beyond just us. Every connection we should have as an evolved and still-evolving organism is critical to our physical, emotional, and spiritual development.

Going out and being connected to nature—looking at the birds, watching the sunset, looking at the stars. These are all part of you interconnecting with the place that you're from. These connect us back to the reality of what we are and who we are.

Being in nature is an exercise in honesty. It reminds us that we're not some "super-meta being" floated in from some place above the clouds.

We all have different ways in which we can connect. Some are pretty particular.

For example, sitting here in the house right now, I don't have the kind of conditions that make me feel complete—I'm not in and on the water as often as I'd like.

But I'm still able to offset the absence of that and what that does to my psyche with intense training, good constructive learning, and hanging out, having friends 'round: uplifting people that are positive and have interesting views and ideas.

I can look to my innovations and developing ideas as a different form of stressing my system.

We need to exercise every aspect of ourselves continuously; and understand that half of the art is in how we calibrate between them.

It's all part of that whole thing. When we remember that everything connects to everything else, we become more vigilant, right? We become able to counteract and recalibrate, using equals and opposites, or other complementary aspects of ourselves and our lives; to ride the stuff that comes our way.

And when I say "whole," I mean in regard to both sides of us. If I just replicated the physicality of being in and on the water, that wouldn't be enough. It would be limiting.

I think because I'm rooted in a very physical world—you know, "Man conquer big wave"—they think, *Oh yeah, surf dude, workout jock. Alpha. He's alpha.*

I just don't do the "alpha male" thing if it's just physical, unfeeling stuff. It's too limiting. I want to develop the whole, and that's about way more than just aggression or strength. That's about true connection. That's about honesty. That's about the connection between the physicality of courage

LAIRD

and the sensitivity of compassion. Nature demands that we understand both of these sides of ourselves—our masculine and feminine sides. That we understand them. And that we connect to them.

If you're turning up with some dumb idea of just being the biggest dog, you might get some scores, some wins, but eventually you're going to fail. Especially if you're taking that into nature. You're turning up with only half the organism.

I suppose, in the world I live in, doing the thing I love is an education in that. I've made that mistake. If you don't bring your whole being to the ocean—if you just bring aggression to the ocean—she'll just hit you right back with it. You can't bully the ocean. You don't "win" with the ocean. You coexist respectfully. Or she'll hurt you.

If you live close to nature—with it—you get that. Hawaiians get that. Hawaiian mysticism has that connectivity right at the heart of it. Connectedness and respect. That's survival. If you have to work with that, with the ocean all around you, it shapes your physicality. It shapes your spirituality.

The ancient Hawaiians believed that all time is now.

They believed that there was one body of life to which they, the land, sea, sky, and on the land belonged.

Everything is connected through the aka threads. These connections can be created with thoughts or intention. *Aka* threads are receptacles and/or conductors for *mana*. They can be activated with attention and sustained concentration.

—CHRISTINA PRATT, *AN ENCYCLOPEDIA OF SHAMANISM*

Consciousness demands connectivity, patience, openness. Physicality is not just about smashing a board into a wave. Or getting ripped to ride it longer.

The ocean needs more—certainly from me. When I'm surfing, my heart does more than just keep the blood in my legs and brain, and keep my centrifuges spinning.

It connects me to the emotion and the energy around me. That's the only way I can do what I do.

Accomplishments, whether they're achieved intellectually, physically, financially, spiritually—they become empty if they are not connected to something bigger. You need to have some humility in there somewhere, or you're screwed.

I have a friend who is a professional athlete. I told him, "If you spend all your time in a stadium with fifty thousand people screaming your name, you better go out and hike awhile; get under a big tree and sit there and be by yourself. That's the only way you can balance out the overwhelming nature of your day job. That is the only way you can offset all that attention and all of that ego and all that stuff."

The only way to do that is to go be solitary: alone. Try to create some balance—try to create some sort of grounding effect; otherwise you will become overinflated by all of that stuff.

You will become like a helium balloon—you'll lose your connection—lose your tie, and just float off.

Our connection to Nature and its ability to heal and help us always goes back to which environment we spent the longest period of time in—the environment in which we spent the majority of our evolutionary time. It's back to that fact, that we spent over 100,000 generations of our evolution in nature.

And that evolution has loaded us with switches, most of

which we have lost the ability to flick. There is so much un-known in us from that time. Protocols, programs, switches.

Nature simplifies things for us. We don't need to decide between science or spirituality with nature. Nature is both, right there in front of us. Nature is everything we know and a lot we still don't, all wrapped up in one big beautiful thing.

We're made of the same things. Ninety-nine percent of our genetic makeup we share with every living organism on the planet, every creature in nature. And that's over time, right? From the beginning to now. And for as long as we exist as a species. We're the same thing. Same particles. Different shapes, perhaps. Different natures. Different func-tions. But the same raw material.

It is us and we are it. In a way, we should look at nature like we're looking in a mirror, right?

Perhaps that's why seeing the state of the oceans is so upsetting for me. Part of me is sick. Part of me is unwell, right? Choking on all that plastic; overfished; ignored. If I use nature as a mirror of myself as a creature, as an organ-ism, I'm hurting.

That's why meditation is so popular. It's a way of an-swering that need for connection, for balance. You take half a second to close your eyes and listen to your breathing, actually feel the organism working.

We need to take the time to picture ourselves as the speck in time we are. The more often we do that, the less surprising it's going to be when we find out there's some-thing way bigger than us. That there's stuff we do know and stuff we don't.

Those brief moments when I . . . am captivated by my sur-
roundings, or when I do nothing more than study a rock with
green moss and find myself unable to pull my eyes away, or
else when I simply hold a child in my arms, are the greatest.

Time is halted and the present is no longer in opposi-
tion to the past and future . . . You experience the fullness
of time in the moment.

—ERLING KAGGE, *SILENCE: IN THE AGE OF NOISE*

But that's the whole "don't shoot the messenger" thing
again. There's a lot of people out there getting physical in
the world—a lot of physicality—which is great: running
marathons, doing peak rides, Iron Man, triathlons, super-
workouts—but it's not really connected. Apart from ego.

It's like, *Nature? Meditation? Not for me. That's just hippie
stuff. Crystals and dream catchers. That's not me. I'm the working
guy, right? Powered up. Doing stuff. In shape. I'm ripped. Got no
time for that connected-to-nature stuff.*

Well, OK, you have no time for that stuff, for nature, for
space—until you get ill, or your mind explodes with all the
bullshit, and believe me, that's going to happen eventually,
unless you're some total psychopath.

And at that point you're either going to get real and start
looking for something more profound, or you're going to
just disappear up your own whatever.

It's not like this stuff is difficult. Meditation can be as
easy as a walk in the park. It can actually *be* a walk in the
park. The smallest thing helps. Just noticing a change in the
seasons. Or the sunlight on a tree. Open up to that. Connect
to that stuff, and life is immediately better.

Nature is in us—and we respond to it measurably. This is not flaky stuff. There are endless scientific and academic papers on the benefits of us being in nature. Nature is part of the brilliant creatures we are.

I see this happen all the time. Whenever we get near nature—especially big nature—waves, mountains, caves—people always are like, "Wow, why am I always feeling like I'm lacking something? I have everything right here. Everything is staring me in the face." That's honesty. The raw, unplugged truth.

What you need is *nothing*—and I don't mean that you don't need anything. I mean what you need is the nothingness that can come from getting out there.

There's a certain aspect of nothingness, when you're on your board out there sitting in the ocean, or in the middle of a forest, or on top of a hill, in a park, whatever. Maybe you have a buddy with you, maybe you don't have a buddy with you, but you put yourself in isolation—you go and subject yourself to isolation—and it's amazingly fulfilling.

Kind of ironic that one of the coolest kinds of connection is when we're disconnecting from everything we usually fill our lives up with. But you're connecting to something far older and deeper.

And you're getting some humility right there. Under that tree. In that park. Looking at the sea, hearing it roar.

You are one organism amongst quadrillions of others, stuck to the surface of a planet that is spinning at 1,200 miles an hour.

And you're traveling at 26,000 miles an hour through a cosmos packed with an infinite source of the light and dark matter that our current understanding tells us we and everything else are made of.

So sure, when you do that, when you are in nature, you're recharging something in the system that you're not getting through all these other things that you're doing—through community, through good lifestyle, good information, good learning.

Isolation, a yearning to get to nature, is the thing you need. Isolation in nature, like with our breath, can deliver its gifts.

"We are confined by what Nature serves us."

—LAIRD HAMILTON

"The one that really gets him—the greatest teacher of all—Mother Nature.

"If she's not delivering, Laird is always confronted with yearning for something; something that he's always waiting for.

"*Will they come again? Will I be able to be in the right spot? Will I be able to perform if I am in the right spot? Is it gonna happen this winter? Isn't it gonna happen?*

"It's a reoccurring theme in his life, which is that there's a part of him always waiting and hoping that the waves come. There's a lot of heartache in that for him. It's a yearning: a constant yearning. Do you know how many fucking times a day Laird looks out and looks to the sea?

"And then there's sort of a knowingness—that he feels that way and that it will happen, but he just doesn't know when."

—GABBY REECE

My feeling is that until we figure this stuff out, we just look at the hole in our lives and fill it in with everything and anything. We're just dumping anything in there that we can, and we don't get the thing that we're needing.

It's interesting to me about how green is a calming color. Green, the signifier of nature, is this magic color to us as a species.

I'm not sure which came first. Does green calm us, so we are attracted to the green of nature? Made aware of it so we tend to it? Or has the fact that we have been in nature for so long made us attracted to green? Who knows.

But I think that once you realize the importance of small things like that—and you just give them a little bit of respect, connect with them—there are remarkable effects to be had.

Like houseplants; like pets; these are ways of us connecting back with nature. We feel better after walking through the park or in the woods because we're amongst friends.

Trees are friends of ours. We are connected to them and they to us in an amazingly simple way. We are part of how each other exists on this planet. We're interdependent—we breathe out what they breathe in; we breathe in what they breathe out. Doesn't get simpler or deeper than that.

The benefits of connectivity are everywhere. Go barefoot for a second. Look at the stars. These are real simple ways for you to reconnect. You'll feel the reward. It's not that hard to implement. That's why breath is so important—because it's an exchange between you and the world around you. That's existence. You're transacting with the cosmos right there—with every breath, you're trading atoms with the cosmos.

So if you're thinking, *OK, this connection thing—I get it,* you might be then wondering how to act on it. Or does it act on you? Does this super-connectivity just happen? Do we wake up one day and go, "Hey, I am so connected." Or do we have to jump-start it?

Well, I think it's a combination of both. But it takes application. You get nothing for nothing. I mean, what's the magic number for truly learning something; ingraining something in you to the degree that it goes from being conscious to unconscious? Ten thousand hours? There's probably something to be said about that.

Having awareness, like awareness of your breath, awareness of your connection—that's the foundation of creating the relationship, reaping the rewards of the understanding.

In the end it goes back to the heart again, because it's back to the fact that intuitively we are connected to the world around us. The electromagnetic field in us connects with those of the organisms around us. We need that connectivity to make us whole, right? Completeness.

It is the relationship between these two aspects—the nature within us and the nature around us, and how they interreact—that shapes our whole. I mean, sure they calibrate slightly differently depending on the situation we're in, but they've got to be engaged—otherwise we're just ticking boxes. We're not expanding out into the world we live in and letting it into us—we're not sharing—we're not reciprocating.

It's a little bit like this: "I follow a diet and I ignore the way the food makes me feel" versus "OK, I'm eating and thinking *that makes me feel all bloated.*" "Oh, *that* makes me feel *this*," you know—I'm responding to it, being sensitive enough to feel it; the effect of it—that's part of it too. But you know, you might have to start with a checklist and then work into the sensitivity of being able to feel it. Simplify stuff.

So breath, awareness, heart, community, all of these dimensions of us firing off each other, that's connectivity for me—not the kind I get through a smart phone.

I think with the digital technological age we're living in right now, we've got a slightly twisted idea of connectivity. And we need to just be conscious of it, be aware of it.

Technology is great, and we've got a load of measurement apps and platforms, right? And we're all sharing this stuff. We're sharing all this data. And there's people running the numbers. Millions of algorithms churning all this data. Setting norms and targets out there.

But we're putting ourselves on a scale that's measured off some weird average: like we're all the same car. Then we're comparing. Comparing everything. Two clicks one way. Five the other. Three points up, four points down.

As far as the numbers are concerned, I'm at my edge; but maybe you're not at your edge. But what does that mean?

Really, I don't think this stuff takes us anywhere in the end.

It's kind of fun, and we play around with it. But actually, knowing if you're at your edge or not? You need to be able to connect with yourself to figure that out. You've got to connect at a deep enough level because, you know, in the end you are the best judge of that.

You are the one deciding, "Hey, this is too hard" or "This is too easy," and not using the scale to do it. I've had times when I'm in the optimum calorie-burning zone and I know it, but I check this with the scale or the measure and it tells me something different.

The confusion or contradiction in some of this stuff. When it feels counterintuitive. You lose me there.

But, more importantly, I guess I kind of lose the point of it all. I think we get too caught up in the details and we forget the objectives. The objective and the detail of the action that you're undertaking have to stay connected, otherwise you just overload.

"It's a little like what in software programming they call 'the kluge'—a phenomenon where you bootstrap another piece of software and then another and then another until eventually you have this juggernaut of inelegance and nonsimplicity. People cease to be able to integrate all this stuff thrown at them. This diet, that regime, this practice, that podcast. We need sustainable processes that are basic and simple. Out of that you can have extraordinary depth of function, based on really simple algorithms. We need to move backwards from complexity."

—KELLY STARRET

There's ways to use technology and quite scientific measurement to help you do stuff.

It's interesting to use different kinds of heart monitors, either to learn to slow your heart rate down way quickly— like as a way to have a reference point, as a way of knowing what protocol you can do to get yourself to drop your heart rate fast—or how high does your heart rate jump up when you're in the sauna?

Those are specific things that you're using to identify or

to confirm: "Hey, so that's how this works" or "Hey, I can do this and *this* happens." There's always a place for instruments, but it has to be linked more with investigation, right?

If it becomes all of what you do—you just collect data all the time off everything, and compare it to anything and everything—if you lose sight of the objective, the instruments have lost their purpose.

But let's be clear here. Tech, and the way innovation has put these super-high-spec instruments into everyone's hands, is game-changing for us as creatures.

It has been one of the most powerful levers in getting a lot of folks off their ass and out into the world.

Take Fitbit and personal-measurement tech—this stuff has inspired millions of people to move—and keep moving, and keep improving. We need as much of that as is possible.

So, say the objective is to ride to the top of the hill as fast as I can—right? And then the details are the things that happen along the way: Where can I go? When can I recover? When can I push hard? All those things. Sometimes we're so caught up in that stuff, that measurement, that smart data, that we forget we're just trying to get to the top of the hill.

I always go back to how we love to disguise imperfection with complexity. If there's a lack of perfection, we just put a bunch of ornaments on it. When your real thing inside is you're just trying to be quick up the hill.

"I live in the human performance world—and the number of pro athletes I see; the university teams I work with; the number of professional organizations and military groups I advise—they're all struggling. The problem with social

LAIRD

media is that we are more distended and disassociated than ever before. So I try to think critically about how we can streamline physical practice to rerun more free time, play time, wonder time—how can we streamline the physical practice?"

—KELLY STARRET

Use instruments and tools to move you through that journey. It's knowing. It's little bits of wisdom to move you along—but make sure those tools and the objective stay connected.

And once you get to the top of the mountain? Take a moment. Don't immediately run down the other side because you got to go and do another one. Take some time. You ride to the top of a mountain to do a certain thing—the only reasons we go there is to rise above stuff. To test ourselves. Take some time. You earned it.

We're losing the ability to take time. Everything is accelerating and the victim is time—and stillness. And ultimately connectedness.

And the irony is, all the stuff that's meant to be speeding us up is often actually creating lag—not removing it.

I was in my car yesterday and I was in the line at the light, and I looked over at the car next to me and there were two people there—and the girl was looking at her phone, and the guy was looking at his phone. And then the light turns green, so I split—but then I look back and they're still sitting there at the light—on their phones—and I felt, like, how is that good? How is that evolving us? We're actually delaying our lives with this stuff half the time.

Technology is supposed to be this thing that's helping us speed up. We're supposed to be becoming more efficient—that's the objective.

But a lot of the time, it just seems to create more delay. Like the delay of email. To have a rigorous conversation on email, I send you an email and I say what I want to say; then you send me an email and say what you want to say. And then by the time we're done with this thing it took a week when, in real human terms, it was a conversation that we could have had in ten minutes on a call—but it was a week.

All these guys out there, in VR and gaming and all that stuff—they're all trying to scrub latency. Lose the lag between command and action. Make everything immediate. No stalling, no glitching, no interference. But it's like that glitching they're scrubbing has to go somewhere—and it's been passed on to us, right? All the tech is rocketing forwards and we're just sitting there buffering.

Let's be clear, technology is amazing. We can't just go, "Oooh, technology, that's bad." That's just lazy thinking and blame-throwing. It's a very human thing we're doing. What we love to do is to take things that are amazing, and abuse them. We just take some amazing stuff and then we abuse it. We junk up on it. We do it with drink, food, everything.

The part of it with my children—that's the scariest part of the whole thing for me. They're from a time where it's always existed. And we don't know the level of impact. We have an instinct. We intuit that it's not all good.

It's a little bit like when cigarettes were cool and it was OK, and everybody was smoking everywhere and everyone's going, "Hey, it's fine." Meanwhile it was just a matter of time before everybody had emphysema and the whole thing was suddenly an epidemic of smoking-related illness.

Where technology is taking us is on another whole level again. Technology is rewiring us. Rerouting neural pathways—from a very, very young age. We don't even understand the implications of it yet. But we do not have the data to prove that it's only a good thing.

My concern is that it's potentially taking us even further away from a state of being that we already are too far away from—we're becoming even less connected. By being more connected, we become less connected. By being faster, we're becoming more delayed. Its classic "light and dark."

At its optimum, technology does this amazing thing. I can see and know all this stuff immediately. I can see the weather for a week—so I can kind of make some plans around it—and I can Google any question I have and somebody will give me some kind of answer, even if it's not the right one.

That's the irony of it—the thing that's so efficient makes for so much inefficiency.

We're going into sign language; now we have emojis. In our pursuit for intelligence we're becoming dumber, and what you notice about the kids—it's less about the *doing*.

They seem to be doing less doing.

We seem to become more complacent with it. You'd think it would motivate us to do more things because you can see so much cool stuff and be like, "Wow, look at this, look at that." But it seems not to have that effect; it seems to make us not even want to leave the couch and go *do* the thing— because we get to *see* someone doing. Vicarious doing.

The smart device is, in many instances, dumbing us— dulling our performance. It also shrinks our world. We forget to look up. We forget to engage. We're just eyes down. Lift your head up. Look where you're going. I find myself victim too. I'm driving down the road and I'm like, *Oh yeah, put that thing down.*

I think we have to make a real conscious effort to put those things down. There's a time and a place and a function—and they're incredible. What you can do is phenomenal—but you need to be able to know how to put them down—we're back to bringing awareness to it.

We are losing ourselves in machines—literally. Our whole identity is not only being formed by them—but hosted by them.

We're giving away responsibility for our identity. We don't want that much work. Human memory? Let me get something that does it for me so I don't have to be responsible for myself. Human memory is going to end up sitting on a billion hard drives and phone storage cards—and no one even looks at this stuff. We're developing Snapchat memories. One minute it's there. Next minute it's gone.

The New York Review of Books has labelled the battle between producers of apps "the new opium wars," and the paper claims that "marketers have adopted addiction as an explicit commercial strategy." The only difference is that the pushers aren't peddling a product that can be smoked in a pipe, but rather is ingested via sugar-coated apps.

—ERLING KAGGE,
SILENCE: IN THE AGE OF NOISE

That's a big part of everything that we do. It's like, "How can I get in shape without working out? How can I get smart without reading books?" We're always looking for the path of least resistance, always, no matter what—in every field. Don't make me eat something that tastes terrible to get in shape. How do I find something that's palatable?

That's the sweet stuff. Sugar in everything. But this isn't just about doughnut and soda advertisments.

The real issue lies with us on that one. Within us— wired into our DNA.

Part of why we're like this is because in nature, sweet tasting? That's safety. Ripened to sweetness. Safe to eat.

In nature, sweet means safe. Again, if we're seeking answers, looking back into our 100,000 generations evolving in nature isn't a bad place to start. We're going back to the switches inside us and we don't even realize that.

Nutritionally, we're still in that mode and we're not going to get out of that gear anytime soon, so we had better learn how to live in it—because you don't just make DNA disappear.

DNA—how we're programmed—doesn't just vanish. It's like making people change so they fit in school. Let's change the student so they fit the school. School's not messed-up. The kids are messed-up. Let's change them. We'll feed the kids Ritalin.

We'll drug them and make them better suited to deal with this stressful environment—and these stressful study programs. Again, this comes down to the disconnect between things.

We respected wisdom once—and we listened to wisdom. And the older generations who carried it. And then we lost wisdom and went for the dollar.

That was when things changed a lot. Suddenly it's like, "OK, well, you may have wisdom but you're in the way of me getting more status, more money, so we got to put you over there. Put you to one side"—instead of "Hey, you have something valuable—and I want to be near it and learn."

OK, there are issues that we have with past generations, some of the stuff they did, being in charge of everything; the world that they lived in influencing how they acted then and still act now.

The world we live in now is not what it was, and a lot of them don't like it—so we marginalize them.

But, that being said, I think a big part of this thing that we're missing is that aspect of respecting our elders, and ultimately learning from their wisdom.

Old people are receptacles of experience. They're hosts of a whole lot of living experiences. And there's no app for that, right? There's no teenage programmer with that much living in the tank. That's the bit we seem to have forgotten. We've gone blind to the fact that in some way, shape, or form, they're a host of a lot of life lessons.

And the genetic thing. If you want to know where you're from, the cultures and social memory you're a living part of—and how you're connected to everything else and how it all works—look to your relatives. Specially the old ones.

Was a time when, if you wanted to know something, anything, there'd be an old aunt or someone that would go, "Oooh, you got a bit of your great-uncle in you," or "your grandfather as a boy."

As humans we need that kind of connectivity. We need that kind of joined-up-ness.

In the end, that kind of connectivity will teach you more about what's important than the smartest phone you can show me.

The meditative response to all of this—what that breath

work does for us, what exercise does for us—they're just the reminder of where we are and who we are—and where we're from. How we've evolved. And we need those reminders; otherwise we get complacent.

That's our evolving intelligence—the knowledge we're collecting—the testing and improving and being more efficient. All that searching for those things, those efficiencies, in order to survive. Searching for those easier ways of collecting and storing stuff.

Our most recent technology has just put that into overdrive. Supercharged it. But there's a downside in there.

It's kind of like macadamia nuts. If I've got to break every one of them, one by one, I only eat so many, and they're precious. They take energy to get. And energy is precious. So they're precious, right?

We're restricted in our ability to overindulge.

But once we've broken that system, once we've industrialized that effort, I can get a big bag of them, and I can store them. I can eat them by the handfuls—until in the end I'm like, "Macadamia nuts? Yeah, whatever."

How would you strip-mine if you didn't have pumps and hoses and pressure? You would just go find gold in the stream, and you'd only find as much as was in the stream, and you wouldn't ruin the ecosystem.

Everybody always loves to say indigenous cultures lived harmoniously with the environment—and I'm like, "Well, yeah and no. They just didn't have the means to mess it up as good as we have."

In his book *Sapiens*, Harari tells us that homo sapiens went to Australia, and within a thousand years of arrival, twenty-five of the biggest mammals that lived there were extinct. So, even in our less-evolved form, we could screw stuff up pretty quickly. We figured out the easy way to get more pretty fast.

You hear things about native Indians, where they didn't do anything that would affect the environment for more than seven generations.

I understand that when you're living in the environment, your relationship is deeper with the environment. You're more concerned with it. But as soon as you start creating houses, structures to live inside, you start to lose that connection.

We insulated ourselves from nature—and as we have done so we have increasingly lost our connection to it, and the intimacy of it, which has made us a lot more reckless.

There's a recklessness that comes from a lack of intimacy, that loss of proximity. It's like, "Out of sight, out of mind."

That's the biggest problem with the ocean—we're just not connected to it. We've surveyed less of the ocean than we have of our galaxy: only 2 or 3 percent of the whole ocean has ever been surveyed. Half the people don't go in it. Or know anything about it. We just dump the shit in the river; the river goes in the ocean. Or we just dump it from a ship, and it just sinks to the bottom.

What is it about us that makes us do the things we do? It's all connected, ultimately. But we forget that. We have to find a way to get reconnected. To get respectful again. To embrace what we know and what we don't know. And respect them both.

This is where the scientific and the spiritual kind of dance, right? But "spirituality" seems like a dangerous word these days.

Anything that accepts that there is something beyond us gets painted as hokey, dumb, or flaky. But we're even failing on the stuff we know. We're even failing in taking notice of the science. Of how everything affects each other. And how once things are connected, they stay connected.

We need to get people to participate in being earthlings— people of the earth, who understand how it works. People who understand how everything connects. How everything is interrelated and interdependent.

For example, we need more people to realize that the air from China takes seven days to get to California. It's all of our air. It's all of our sea. All of our trees. All of our mountains. The ecosystems of the world are interconnected and interrelated.

So my own idea is this: the more we can have people go swimming in the ocean, the more people will be concerned about how the ocean is—so if I can get a load more people out there using paddleboarding, or using kitesurfing, I'm going to do it.

We need to get our heads around this. We need to use the brilliant technology and connectivity we have created to connect every human being to the oceans that spawned us, at every opportunity—to help them understand that their relationship with it, and to it, is sacred.

But we also need to get our face out of these screens for ten seconds and look up and around us to see what the hell's going on. Everything's trying to give us clues. The weather is trying to tell us something. We're just too wrapped up in stuff, too wrapped up in ourselves to care that much.

Remember, evolution is smarter than us. And evolution is not the sole privilege of our species. If we're not careful, a really smart, highly evolved planet is going to purge itself of humans. Like, *Thanks guys, but we're good here. You can go.*

"We have to work towards the unification of knowledge, we have to integrate these practices into a sustainable whole. You can't always go to a week-long retreat and have some-one make your meals and lead you by the hand. You have to go home and figure out how all this stuff works in the context of real life. What I love about Laird and Gabby is that they've done that. They're not monks; they work harder and longer than anyone I know, they have their kids, they have five businesses, and they don't fuck around with the things that make all that possible."

—KELLY STARRET

We need to keep evolving and learning and growing. And we need connectivity to do that. We need the friction of experience. It's kind of like building a statue that you've been chipping away at. You're not sure which chip created the shape because there's a bunch of chips.

But the ones that keep you humble, being thankful and appreciative—and also maybe being a little more methodi-cal about when you approach things, a little less reckless in your approach—the things that saved you along the way: these are the ones that shape us.

And you have to feel this. You can't just think it. Mak-ing decisions using only reason, never engaging instinct or intuition—that makes no sense to me.

As I said before, the book *Natural Born Heroes* says the one key emotion is compassion.

You can't be truly heroic without being compassionate. Period. Anybody that does anything heroic has to be compassionate. And compassion, I would say, is more of a feminine trait.

The accomplishment of an ego is limiting. Accomplishment of your spirit and your soul is far more fulfilling.

As I found out, you can achieve the greatest thing ever—something you've waited your whole life for—but if you're heartbroken, it means nothing.

That's perspective. Achievement should be about family, friends. Those are achievements.

I've felt that. I know. Jaws [the surf break at Pe'ahi, Maui] was that moment for me.

The other side of us, for males particularly, is connected back to hunting. We get hung up on achievement. Achievement is our prey. We caught the big game—whatever the modern-day version of a successful hunting journey is—and there is glory in that, but at the end we have to have a village waiting for us. We have to have a family waiting for us. Otherwise, what's the point? Empty glory is a lonely feeling.

That's why so many people that achieve a lifelong goal are depressed and let down at the end—because they're missing the completeness it takes to make it really fulfilling—truly, spiritually fulfilling. Some people have different versions of what they need, but that's what I've found with most guys I know. That's the truth.

I know my mind is connecting more these days to family and, obviously, to my relationship with the woman I love. But all of it, whether you have it be your friends or your peers or your teammates, whatever connects to the wholeness of everything—that's riches. That's achievement.

"I think because of the experiences he went through, Laird had a hard time trusting people.

"He continued to be tested and people kept trying to pick on him all the way to high school—but if you go back to these people, the ones he got into a fight with, I can guarantee they have had a change of heart. I think they would look at him respectfully as a Hawaiian warrior. So Laird in a sense has gained respect from everybody."

—COPPIN COLBURN

Ultimately, why am I here? To experience—to experience all of it, right?

Your hope is that you learn the lessons so you can avoid certain experiences, those experiences that aren't productive. That's what learning should be—we need to experience everything.

What those experiences are is totally unknown—at any point in our lives there are unknowns. Things we are yet to experience. The incomprehensible. The things beyond us—until they happen.

For every single person it's something unique. You can't compare your experience to mine, and I can't compare mine to his.

So the Why, for me? The Why is to be human and experience everything—to experience what being human is. In my world that's my relationship with the ocean, family, with my children, my friends, my feelings—and I mean *every* feeling.

Feelings of *Wow, my friends and I are better friends than we've ever been. My family's good. My family's bad. My kids are*

OK. My kids aren't OK. I'm strong. I'm not strong. I'm injured. I'm not injured. I rode a big wave. I didn't ride a big wave.

Everything connects you to who you are. Even what you're not good at connects to the stuff you are.

"If you cut Laird in half and looked at the rings, they're all the same. There is no wobble. He is who he is through and through, and that doesn't change from one day to the next. That's it. His integrity is to the core. That's something I'd like to strive more greatly for."

—KELLY STARRET

I suck at stuff that I'm not intrigued by. The problem is, I am only intrigued by things that I'm good at. So I always try to work on trying to be better at things that I'm not good at. My perspective is that I can always be better at everything.

Maybe that's it. Maybe that's my friction. My dynamic tension. Maybe I'm not good at thinking I'm so good at stuff. That I'm incapable of really being content with things that I'm good at—which can be obnoxious. It's brutal, because you're always doubting, no matter what people do and say.

Any goal is almost unachievable, because I can't get to it—because it's always moving—because even if I get to it, I think I didn't do it good enough or I could do it better.

If I had been in school in California now, they'd have ten abbreviated definitions for all my issues and they'd probably be trying to put me on Ritalin or something. But the question then is: Is this a natural trait? Is it in the organism? Or is it learned? Nature or nurture, right?

There's a long list, but the main one? I'm not good at being able to change my addictive personality—I'm not good at that. But it is connected to what I've achieved. To everything I am.

I'm fortunate that I've been able to avoid putting negative things on me. It's not like I'm a drug addict. My addictions are healthy. I'm a health food addict, I'm a surf addict. But again, if I was looking for a thread that tied all this stuff together, I think the main one is: I always just never felt good enough. Always thinking: *Could I be stronger? Could I be faster?* It's exhausting. But I've gotten better at it, in the sense that I still don't necessarily sit back, but I also don't put the amount of doubt or negativity on it that I probably did when I was younger.

Again, I'm hoping that I'm learning. I think what happens is that over time you just realize the unproductiveness of it; the waste of energy. You realize that it's not worth putting that negative energy into life. It's a balance.

I think I've begun to learn how to tap into my energy without always having to get it from something outside, even if it's the ocean.

I'm a lot nicer person for it. At a certain point you get an idea of what it takes for you to get some sort of balance, and that part of it. And that's the circle of life right there.

You went out into the world to find that the things you needed were at your house already. And you realize that you're connected by things you never realized. And that some stuff isn't as important as you thought it was. Like the ocean.

That's quite a strange thing for me—to have got so much power from it, and one day you go, "Actually, I'm good with that." That can be confusing. Because at a certain point, that's the thing that kept you there, the thing you need—it's part of your identity. It *is* your identity. And then suddenly, one day, it's not so important. That's the journey.

I don't think I'm done with the ocean. Or that it isn't still a big part of my identity. But for a long time there was an aspect of Jaws that was connected to my identity. I needed to go back to Jaws and ride the waves and show people what I could do—and get my identity from that. So I did.

In the process of going in and doing it, I've been able to be OK with that. I've come to peace with it. I don't have to go do that again. I'm good with it. I'm not the boxer that has to be punched until he can't get up. I don't need to do that.

"On Kaua'i, Laird just does his stuff. Pretty ordinary. Pretty invisible existence. But you know—he had to do something so radical and be recognized for it—to become that invisible—to level the playing field.

"Sure, the *ha'ole* thing pops up sometimes. But I've seen him in the last few years almost transcending that. I think he's kind of made a sense of peace. I think he sees it; understands it.

"But for the most part—he's had to get some pretty extreme accolades just to kind of cruise through on the island. Just to be invisible."

—GABBY REECE

But I can see how that can happen—if everything was still connected to that—if that still defined me, consumed me, I would have peace with it. But again, it gets back to family and friends and that whole part where you gain something so much more profound when you get beyond these things. You climb to the ridge and then see this bigger thing.

You realize that you represent something to your community—your tribe. When you represent something to your tribe, whatever that looks like—that helps to shape your identity as well, and then it becomes less about achievement, and then it's more just about where you are in the group—that you represent something that's important to the group.

The thing that connects you is just being a valuable part of that tribe. Maybe that's all I wanted. That's family. That's *'ohana*. In the end. That's connectivity.

Barefoot Business

Everything Is Connected

The most enlightened and successful entrepreneurs and business leaders understand that we live in a world stitched together to a staggering degree by accelerating technology and hyper-connectivity.

Every aspect of a business affects every other. The old world of silos—departments not talking or collaborating—is a relic: the vestigial tail of twentieth-century business.

Modern businesses, from the smallest start-up to the largest multinational, operate in a world where interrelatedness, interdependence, and integration are the order of the day—not just as an economy and efficiency drive to scrape the margin and reap more profit, but to create a truly standout business. The truly great business leaders have an innate and intuitive sense of this, and act upon it with fierce application.

How the business co-creates with its peers and partners; how it collaborates with others in the sector; how it balances and calibrates regulatory governance and product focus in the predominating customer-first culture; how it values and tends to every spoke in its wheel—its people, purpose, commitments, ambitions, its duties both to the immediate communities from which it draws support and resources, and to the wider world in which it seeks to thrive—these things make the difference between success and failure.

Here, Laird and Gabby explore the threads of their businesses, and how they manage the checks and balances of each business in relation to the others, and in light of their ethos and beliefs.

LAIRD

In order to go out there and be totally engaged and clear, and be optimum—to be out there totally unencumbered—you have to have everything be OK. All of those pieces have to be together. There has to be some harmony going on.

Doesn't matter whether the body is an individual or a company. Same rule applies.

I've tried being my best when I've been disconnected. I know what that's like. I know how that can affect you—and sometimes it's not even obvious. It just comes from somewhere unseen. And sometimes it comes from obvious stuff: I'm not getting along with my family or my wife or my kids, and something's going on and I'm out there, and that's in your head, and that's blocking you from what you need to do. Sometimes it's not so obvious—sometimes you're just not settled. You're not settled completely, and I think for me personally, I feel like there's a spoke in the wheel that will stop it rolling perfectly.

Everything is connected to everything else. No point pretending it isn't. As in business, as in life.

When one or two or three of the spokes on that wheel are a little loose or a little too tight, then there's a break in the roll. The roll doesn't flow nicely when everything's slightly at odds with itself. Your business life is no different to your personal life in that.

And it can take the smallest imbalance to create that. When everything's right, then you're able to perform—you're free, you're not encumbered, you're not blocked—you have the potential to perform optimally. In business, the phrase "fit for purpose" applies as much to the directors, the managers, and the founders and the owners, as it does to the products or the services they're selling.

You can't seek optimum performance and not tend to every spoke to get it. You can't get to optimum if you don't care for the people you work with—the relationships you make.

You can't expect to get the best out of people if you don't understand what they do every day, and respect it.

You can't expect to have the openness and generosity that collaboration and innovation need in one area, and not give a shit in another—be mean-spirited or uncaring in the impacts of what you're doing on the planet or on people, or whatever.

The businesses you run are either true to that or they're not. If your businesses have some toxic shit going on in them, or you're creating or generating bad stuff in pursuing those businesses, that's going to reduce your performance. That's going to suck out the success.

And there's a lot of industry out there ignoring those signs. They are big enough to have lost their connection with really important stuff.

That's why we have so much industry dodging the bullet for what they do in the world. All in the name of success.

And it's going to be hard to reconcile that—and I think that the overwhelming aspect of the level of our destruction and our abuse of the environment means that we're not optimum.

What we've done to this planet we're flying around on—and the levels to which we've done it and the volume of that—it's industrial, what we've done.

What we've done and still do to our environment, the impacts on it at an industrial level, at such a mass level in every quarter? That is something that business, and the people who run those businesses, must be held accountable for.

What's the saying? "For what does it profit a man to gain the whole world and lose his soul?"

What's the point? A pile of money, or shares, or another club membership? Or a bigger company?

But you know, half the problem is, if you think you're going to be long dead when the shit comes down, and you're self-interested, I suppose you just don't care.

So for me, in business as in life, everything is connected. You just need to care. It's always back to care. And compassion. And true leadership. There's a lot of fake leadership out there in business. A lot of posturing. No care. No compassion.

GABBY

My role in Laird's businesses is that of an adviser—someone who understands business and intimately understands every aspect of Laird. Because it means I can join the dots on Laird—connect the seen and unseen stuff that perhaps an agent or manager might not know.

If I only understood Laird and didn't understand business, it would be much harder for business teams to work with the two of us together—whatever the business is, whether it's superfood, apparel, or XPT. I suppose it's down to me to understand the business dynamics and what makes them work—and then apply what's needed from Laird in the best way.

The intimacy, the responsibility for his integrity, is critical to this.

You have to consider the person the whole time you're doing it—and just because it's a good idea doesn't mean it's a good idea for the person; or it may not be the biggest idea, but it's a really good idea for the person.

I suppose what he's saying through our partnership is, "I'm going to trust you because you've shown me that I can trust you."

Laird gives absolute trust to me in determining new opportunities.

And I am responsible for him being OK with stuff. And I'm responsible for putting the right team around something.

I'm responsible for keeping this stuff authentic and real to him.

So, for example, we had this one deal that on the surface of it sounded really great. We had got these guys who were really credible—but I knew I was in over my head. So I brought in James, an adviser of ours, because I knew there was some new stuff in there; some new aspects that I knew I was going to miss.

That's part of that role, right—who's the right team at the right time?

But the ability to make the decision, the ultimate decision, that's with me.

I am the one who ultimately sits there and goes: "This is the opportunity; these are the positives and negatives; this is how much time it'll take from Laird; this is what we anticipate, the upside being this—and this is how it fits into the whole ecosystem," at which point I may well go, "OK, on balance, it's probably one not worth pursuing at this time," and that decision kind of gets made unilaterally, by me.

That's the trust he has.

He'll be surfing, come back, and either there's a deal done or there's not—if there's not, then we haven't wasted his time bandwidth.

So my role is very different to that of an agent or a business manager—for two reasons, I think. One, because of the intimate understanding of the person; and two, because of the understanding of business. Laird can understand if a deal is right for a person, or if the economics are going to make sense—but a sponsorship or an endorsement deal—that's not his thing.

And I'm not interested in getting a "yes" just for immediate impact or advantage. The advantage I get to have is that I can say, "Hey Laird, this is going to take a little time—there's not going to be any upsides for you right away—but in the big picture, this is important."

With many agents, if people are not immediately valuable to them and what they are doing, sometimes they don't even call people back.

We've had that. And after I heard about the twentieth person say, "You know, we tried to get ahold of you for such and such, but just got no response from your agent"—I was done.

You call people back—even if it's a "no." You treat people professionally—even if it's a nineteen-year-old college student that wants to interview Laird on his Podcast that has 612 listeners. I will say, "You know what? Laird really appreciates being invited, but he doesn't have the bandwidth now."

Because I believe, big and small, you've got to get back to people and respond to people. You know what? It takes five minutes—and even if it's like, "Hey, no, it's not going to happen"—at least you're treating them with respect.

Because that stuff comes back around. Goes around, comes around. So you need to make sure that when it does come around, it's good. Because everything is connected.

Connect the Dots

"Everything is connected" could be viewed as a trite synopsis of life and how we ride it. But for it to be trite would require it to be a truth that everyone is broadly aware of and actively engaged in applying in life, to the point of banal repetition. But we aren't. Not by a long shot. We are splintering ourselves across more and more personas and threads and environments and communities, eschewing old solid structures in favor of liquid modernity. This is due to a number of things: the natural decay and decline of the old ordering systems we once relied upon (religion, feudal hierarchies, political systems, and economic models); the immediate-gratification culture that sets strict frameworks aside as inconvenient and obstructive; and easy access to technologies, platforms, and systems that allow us to hurtle through multiple lives without the friction of overbearing structures to get in our way. But to Laird's mind, what has developed in this hyper-connected vacuum is, in human terms, the wrong kind of connectivity. Technology must be in service to the human and not the other way around. It is a supplement to consciousness—an accelerator and elevator of it. But it is not a proxy for it.

As Laird points out, we are still a million miles away from technologies being "human." To call them "human" is to claim sentience for them. Algorithmic filtering and curating of data and information, and the mimicry of human response mechanisms, are not sentience. Human grammar is something that perhaps machines can parse. But feeling and sentience remain *unknown unknowns* to technologists. To be human is our mantle and ours alone.

Laird's idea of super-processed connectivity does not lie in a piece of code or an algorithm: It lies in the brilliant kaleidoscope of interactivity that exists between individual human beings—and in the genetic red threads that bind us to every other animate creature on the planet: It lies in the systems our own organism is running and how those systems interrelate with each other internally, and also with the world about us externally. It lies in how we meaningfully engage in relational terms to our kin and our children—and our connection to the community around us and the environment in which we collectively exist: And it lies in the irrepressible connection between our collective human nature and the natural capital of the planet on which we rely.

In Laird's world, connectivity is a primal fabric that technology only supplements, and weakly at that. For Laird, we need to tend to the stuff built over hundreds of thousands of generations, not just decades. That is the only way in which we "join the dots"—in which we can find **balance**. And ultimately it is perhaps the one way we can not only understand our place in the world, but also secure it, and thereby find a sense of **belonging**. And in those two words we find our final threads.

BALANCE

"Balance" is such a loaded word. For some it is nirvana. But equally, for others, it is little more than a circus trick. An exercise in whimsical language. Or a trending mindfulness or tantric gimmick.

But even if we look squarely and cynically (in its purest sense) at the idea of balance—through the lens of what we have explored and revealed in our conversations with Laird—we see a very basic human need, physically, emotionally, environmentally, mentally, and spiritually. It is the furthest thing from some elevated state. It is actually one of the most basic requirements for survival. Whether we are seeking to hang our human hammock between science and spirituality, or walk the path between chaos and order, or navigate a road between technological living and analogue being, balance is essential. And to do that we have to have considered the interrelatedness and interdependence of all things.

BELONGING

Why are we here? What's our purpose? What are we doing? What's the point? These existential human questions are rooted in a concern about "not belonging." *Should I be here? Do I deserve to be here? Do I have a role?* At a universal level they are questions focused not only on *"Why* do I belong here?" but also on *"How* do I belong here?" It's an unsurprising concern. Belonging is core to our humanity, our social sense of self, and how our nature and actions and being validate our existence.

For Laird, this has a very simple baseline. To even raise these questions—to even be allowed a moment to consider them—we have to have survived. We have to have found a way to reward our endeavors with the luxury of time to think about these things, uncluttered by the danger or fear of hunger, homelessness, famine, flood, poverty, disease, and war. And that only comes with us having fulfilled a succession of relentless *doing*. The irony is that to even consider questions of belonging, we must have already committed to it. We need to have committed to participating in the life in front of us—regardless of higher-order existential questions and concerns.

Belonging, for Laird, is about survival with "stickers." Survival with a few gold stars of recognition for embracing the most human life we can. Belonging is to have not only stayed in the game in our competition with death, but to have done so without losing our sense of what makes us human—without losing our brilliance and compassion.

'Ohana

In the Hawaiian belief system, everything is connected in Oneness—the fourth level of awareness—*ike papakauna*. That connection reaches from inside every person to the furthest corners of their universe through the *akai* threads.

One of the principle strengths of *'ohana* is that it makes brothers and sisters of us all, whether related by blood or experience or purpose. Everyone, much as everything in the world, is connected in our journey. Family members and close friends are connected to each other as well as to the immortals, like the *'aumakua*, or family god.

And in a world where all time is Now, the *'ohana* members of the past and the future share the same universe.

The connection between the Hawaiian people and their immediate environment, the natural world in which they dwell, and the cosmos around them is absolute.

Their connection to the land is a source of enormous pride and history—hence the name *'keiki o ka'āina,* or children of the land. Combine this with their conservational nature—as much about respecting the universe and natural world that has come before them as about nurturing the one that is yet to be—and then set a line that runs up from the lower to the middle and then the upper soul, and the model of Oneness takes shape.

Imagine that the *'ohana* stands at the center of a large sphere, and the space within that sphere represents "all time."

Trace a line from the furthest point behind the *'ohana* to the furthest point ahead of it; this marks time from its beginning to its end. Then imagine circles radiating horizontally outward from the *'ohana,* connecting it to its immediate environment, to community, and to the edges of the natural world and the cosmos beyond. And then imagine a line running up through the middle of the *'ohana* from the bottommost point of the sphere beneath them to the highest point above them—and on that line are mapped the three levels of consciousness connecting the lower, middle, and upper souls.

If we start to visualize *'ohana* at the center of Oneness in that way, there is a completeness in this view of Being where everything is connected: interrelated, integrated, and interdependent.

An Exercise in Connecting the Dots

In *Liferider* terms, the simplest way to join the dots is perhaps to look at the points of focus we have explored and revealed.

Commitment drives performance, which in turn provides

the proof that leads to trust; and humility fires compassion, which in turn fuels reciprocity—an empathetic, sympathetic human exchange. And through reciprocity we find balance, and through trust we find belonging.

So, finding ways of exercising these aspects of ourselves is key to a more contented and shared life. But again, the question is: How can we move from some vaunted theory into an everyday fact—a set of acts that we can undertake wherever we are in the world, and whosoever we are?

Laird has a simple set of exercises to address this question every day, regardless of where he is and what he is doing. A succession of three simple actions to prime the day in a joined-up way:

FIRE UP. FUEL UP. OPEN OUT.

FIRE UP is about triggering the organism's external sensors and internal systems, sharpening us up to engage with the day. This involves temperature. At the end of your hot shower, turn it to cold. And stay there. Count to 120. Stay fixed underneath it. Allow your system to recalibrate—to go from the shock of the cold to a more even, sharpened feeling inside and out.

FUEL UP is about setting the dial with the first things you consume in the day. For Laird, this is nonnegotiable. Caffeinate. With a creamer to temper the caffeine spike and even out the energy release. Then eggs, perhaps. With rye toast. No piles of cereal drenched in Bovine Growth Hormone—or wheat toast—to bloat the machine. Keep it lean.

OPEN OUT is about compassion—putting some love in the room. A kiss. A hug. Some physical demonstration of your connection and commitment to someone other than yourself. To your child, your partner, your friend, a family pet. Everything and anything that fires and fills your heart is good. This puts your heartful, reciprocal, and compassionate self in the room. You're good to go.

And you haven't even left the house yet!

Epilogue: The Sea

"If the sea was above us, perhaps we'd take more notice."

—LAIRD HAMILTON

WE began this book at the end, with death, and we shall end it at the beginning: at the place where life began.

At the heart of Laird, and at the heart of *Liferider*, sits one immutable, irrepressible, powerful truth: a truth connected both to where we've come from and to where we're going as a species.

The sea.

From our past to our future, the oceans and seas of the planet on which we've evolved are written through our human existence—biologically, physiologically, physically, emotionally, and ultimately, spiritually.

From the invisible and the banal to the breathtaking and the remarkable, they are interrelated and intertwined with every aspect of our existence.

Our genes are littered with the evidence of a degree of evolutionary intimacy with the seas that even now is only just beginning to be revealed.

Since the oral tradition and storytelling began, the sea has played a central role in the development of our psyches, venerated by philosophers, writers, poets, musicians, and artists alike.

The oceans color the myths and legends that formed our cultures and civilizations. They have provided the material of adventure and heroism, and of darkness and fear.

They are the light and dark of us, and we exist in their gift.

If we don't find a way to stabilize—if not reverse—what's going on in our oceans, and quickly, the danger will be that we are left with the "flat planet" of Laird's nightmares—the oceans laid low: moribund, stagnant, suffocated, and stilled. We will have to come to terms with the fact that we effectively helped to kill the thing that we love. And watermen like Laird will have to come to terms with their memories finally becoming bigger than their dreams—because the future will no longer hold the waves and the connectedness and the richness of the oceans that once powered their imaginations.

LAIRD

It's going to be hard to reconcile what we're doing and have done to the oceans.

To fix it, we're just going to have to prioritize; just because of the sheer scale and connectedness of it all.

One of the lessons from climatic history is that there is no period in Earth history that we know about where the rate of rise of atmospheric CO_2 is as great as it is today. Human beings are truly carrying out a global experiment involving an unprecedented level of interference with the natural system.

—PETER WADHAMS,
A FAREWELL TO ICE

We evolved out of the earth's oceans—the primordial soup. We should be more connected with this stuff.

Something like 70 percent of the earth's oxygen is produced by phytoplankton in the sea—by one-cell organisms. They do all the heavy lifting out there—but everyone's going, "Well, what about the ozone layer, what about global warming and the atmosphere?" and I'm saying yes, they're important—but the atmosphere and the ozone layer are important for other reasons.

But those organisms in the sea absorb something like 50 to 80 percent of carbon. The oceans absorb over half of the stuff humans emit every year, in terms of carbons. The Southern Ocean alone absorbs something like 20 or 25 percent of our emissions. That makes it a pretty important piece of the global weather puzzle.

The Southern Ocean has got a big, really important thing that it does as part of how the ecosystems of our planet connect and work—as part of the thing that keeps the air we're breathing breathable. So that's the question. How do we prioritize the right stuff and act?

There are a couple of projects that are interesting to me. There's this one that I got exposed to called Project Zero—where they have begun to try to prioritize what things are important, because a lot of things don't matter if the other things don't happen.

It's an earth thing—the ocean and the earth are one. Everything is connected. It's the earth; it's the weather; it's the melting of the caps—all of this—every single thing is tied back to the ocean.

And we're going to struggle to try to hold on and protect the few remaining sanctuaries that are left in the ocean.

And at a certain point, if we try to assert some form of meaningful control, it's going to take an army to defend the ocean—it's going to need to get military.

We'll fire rockets and bombs to protect what we think is precious. What about the ocean—the most precious thing we have?

Realistically, to stop shark finning and whale killing, and mass illegal fishing, and then all the casual mass-polluting, we are going to need to get military.

But this is just one side of it.

Because even with all that being said, and even with a militarized ocean protection system, you still have the temperatures rising because of the globe warming up, and water levels are rising with them. We'll be lucky if we can focus on trying to make a few of the ocean species left survive.

I don't say I give up hope, because I don't ever give up hope, but it's just that my desperation gets to the point where I think the best I can do is to make people be in awe of it—and then also get people to participate in being in it, so that they care—you know, because if you don't care, you don't act.

And we need knowledge here. Information. A lot more information.

How can you protect something you don't know anything about? We've only explored like 3 percent of the ocean, or some crazy thing—but we've killed 90 percent of the fish.

I feel that everyone can play a part, however small, in creating the scale of change we need; not using a couple of plastic bags, and not drinking out of plastic straws, isn't going to do it.

When I went into the Gulf and I flew over that place after that giant oil spill, it was devastating. We're not supposed to be drilling into the core of the planet a mile below the ocean—what are we doing? The volume of destruction and contamination—the scale of it is the part that's hard to grasp.

It's not just the oceans—it's every river that runs into them—and what we allow to feed into those rivers from the industries on their banks.

So all I can do is help to bring people to the oceans.

Being in it and caring for it—in that way participating with it and engaging with it; that's the beginning of some understanding, at least.

Then understanding leads to the prioritization of what's important, and then supporting and acting on those things.

But these are scale issues. There are some people who are working on particular aspects. For example, there's some research going on where they are trying to create coral that can live in warmer water, but are we going to just keep re-pollinating the ocean with coral? I have hope, but these are things of such mass scale.

And the scale demands that everyone has to come together—to act as one. The more we keep on feeding disagreement, the longer we'll take to all agree on doing anything. In this way, the skeptics are destroying action.

Let's be clear here.

If you want to figure out the coral situation, then you need to figure out the ocean situation; and to figure *that* out, you have got to figure out how to not let the planet get hot—that's about the level of it.

If you're really concerned about the ocean, the real thing that's going to help the ocean is to figure out how to chill the planet down—because the heat of the planet is going to heat the water up, and it's going to kill all the coral.

So figure that out. Meaningfully. And there needs to be some hard-and-fast rules.

First of all, no one should be able to kill any sea mammal. Period. Start at the top and then we can go from there.

I mean, that's why Sea Shepherd and some of these other guys—they're out there trying to sort some answers—but this is governmental-level stuff. NGOs and action groups are ultimately not the lever here. This is political.

To enforce this, at a certain point, we're going to need to recognize and apply a formal geopolitical status. The ocean needs to be a country, it needs to have flag—and it needs a military.

We need both hard and soft power at work here.

We need red lines. *Do not go there. Do not do this. Or there will be a consequence.* Hard power that takes action.

And we need soft power. We need acceptance, understanding, and compassion. We need to understand how everything is connected to each other, and how we are connected to it. A part of it.

The Pacific is by no means a landless, uninhabited ex-
panse. It is studded with twenty-five thousand islands,
large and small, each with its own stories, of people,
and animals. Their narratives crisscross the ocean in an
embroidered web, drawn together in invisible lines of
connection from shore to island to sea, transversed in
ancient feats of navigation and migration that put our
modern, computer-assisted efforts to shame. Here the
remotest journeys ended; and here many began, too.

—PHILIP HOARE, *THE SEA INSIDE*

But me, Laird Hamilton, alone? I couldn't support
enough charities and do enough that needs to be done. But I
appreciate being asked.

Somebody wanted me to go and talk to the UN on this.
People are beginning to notice, people are starting to care,
but for some of the issues it's a little late—and things are
only getting more complicated and harder to unpick by
the day.

The Great Pacific Garbage Patch—that's a really tricky
one, because that has so much biological stuff wrapped up in
it that it makes it almost impossible to do anything simply.

But we have incredible technologies and an amazing
ability to innovate—and we have some very smart people
in the world. If we can get them to focus on that subject, it
would be enormously productive.

But we need to help people on this journey. You can have
all the brilliance and technology in the world, but if it comes
to a country surviving or not—people eating or not—then

they're just going to take what they think they need to take, and do what they need to do.

If I can't eat? Or I'm struggling? Please don't even talk to me about ocean welfare. I'm looking out for my own, right?

But it isn't just basic needs and the politics of making this stuff fairly available to people. This stuff is being driven by consumption. This is about people just wanting stuff. Just endless stuff. This is about us consuming luxuries far beyond our basic needs of food and warmth and shelter.

Humanity needs to make its mind up. And the people at the top have to help humanity do it.

In the end, is it survival of individual interests? Or is it survival of the oceans?

History tells us we're going to always pick our own survival. We need to somehow stop that being our reflex response. Because survival of the species should top that, right? And we're going nowhere as a species if we don't sort this stuff out.

"We must put aside short-term national gain to prevent long-term global catastrophe. Conserving our oceans and using them sustainably is preserving life itself."

—UN SECRETARY-GENERAL ANTÓNIO GUTERRES

We need to help people not be put in a position where they're having to choose—having to make sense of that. Because left to our own devices, we don't always make the best decision. There is only one real choice for us.

Caring is everything. And if we don't, who will?

LAIRD

"It gives him great gifts—because of his dedication. One time somebody told me a story. They saw Laird at Point Dume [a surf break in Malibu] and he was surfing. They saw a bunch of dolphins near him, and Laird took his wedding band and banged it on the surfboard—and then a wave came and it took him, standing up, and in the wave were the entire pack of dolphins jumping all around him, real close, up by his head. That's a really profound thing. Those are gifts to Laird."

—GABBY REECE

It's back to that thing we talked about—about us being earthlings. We are it. It is us. We've got to care about this stuff because this stuff is connected. It's all connected.

And if we lose the ability to be part of that—if we lose the ability to connect to everything nature has to bring us, and to everything that nature has put inside us—if we lose the ability to connect to the life we have—to commit to it heart, body, and soul—it's not just the oceans that are going to suffer. Everything suffers, right?

We're in competition with death. And death's going to win in the end, right? So let's make the time we have worth it. For me, that's why we're here. To live the fullest life. To feel everything, every gift that being human brings to us. To do everything we can do, to feel everything we can. If we can do that, then we've lived. That's a life.

ACKNOWLEDGMENTS

LAIRD HAMILTON

I would like to thank Julian for his tireless work and investigative approach to the material; William Cawley for being a constant source of ideas, creativity, and support; Jennifer Cawley for her beautiful art and the ability to get me to do anything and barely notice. Thanks to Gabby for her continued love and support and for being such a great partner in this journey; to Bela, Reece, and Brody, whom I love and adore and who are the greatest teachers of all (besides the ocean).

JULIAN BORRA

With greatest thanks and appreciation for the inspiration, patience, and insights of Laird and Gabby Reece, who allowed me into their lives and homes to climb under the skin of this endeavor; for the personal contributions and reminiscences of Coppin Colburn, Terry Chung, Randall Wallace, and Kelly Starret; for the creative partnership, collaboration, and contributions of William and Jennifer Cawley in the "doubting hours"; for the researching rigor of Katerina Cerna in making sense of my ramblings; for the reader's insight of Vivienne Parry OBE, Kelly Myer, Randall Wallace, and Dr. Andy Saulter. And finally, the greatest acknowledgment must go to the sun and the moon of my life, Livia and Louis, by whose rising and setting I navigate this life.

ALSO BY

LAIRD HAMILTON

AVAILABLE EVERYWHERE BOOKS ARE SOLD

RODALE.
BOOKS